# COLOR, TEXTURE, AND PATTERN 4

# DECORATING MATERIALS, TOOLS, AND SUPPLIES 18

# PREPARATION 40

# BASIC PAINTING TECHNIQUES 56

# WALLPAPERING BASICS 72

# COLOR, TEXTURE, AND PATTERN

Color, texture, and pattern are three of the most powerful and cost-effective decorating tools. If you understand the rules that govern each, you can bring beauty and harmony to your home's interior. While plain white walls may be a good choice in some decorating schemes, too often rooms are painted white because it's the easiest choice. If you want to bring a little more pizzazz to your home, this chapter will show you how to incorporate color, texture, and pattern into your interior decorating scheme. You'll learn how to avoid common mistakes so that you can express your own sense of style with confidence and skill, giving your home a personal look.

*Earth tones on the walls and ceiling combine with the light-colored wood flooring and cabinetry to make this living room a cool, calm retreat.*

*Subtle stripes on the salmon wallpaper lend visual texture to these bedroom walls without making them seem busy.*

Deep pink walls look warm and cheery in this family room. White painted woodwork sets off the walls.

Grass cloth, a wallcovering of loosely woven fibers, brings texture and color to the walls in this sitting room.

## MEET THE WALL WIZARD

Learning how to paint a room and put up wallpaper could be about as much fun as watching the paint and paste dry. Unless, that is, you learn from Brian Santos, the Wall Wizard.

In his popular painting and papering demonstrations, presented at home and garden shows around America, Brian teaches techniques and tricks of the trade that help homeowners complete their projects easily and with pro-quality results.

"My mission is to educate people," the Wizard says. He delights in entertaining people while he teaches them too. In this book, the Wall Wizard delivers in-depth information on every aspect of painting and wallpapering, including advice on how to choose colors and make decorating decisions.

"Paint and wallpaper manufacturers put out great products," Brian says, "but they don't really tell people how to use

them properly. Anyone can pick up a brush—I want to help people achieve great results when they do."

A fourth-generation decorative artist, Brian learned a wealth of classical painting and wallpapering techniques from his father and grandfather. "The changes you make with paint or paper are immediate and magical—I was filled with wonder at this from childhood," the Wall Wizard says.

Brian teaches straightforward, proven techniques that take the myth and mystery out of painting and wallpapering. By explaining the logic behind the processes, he helps people build the self-confidence it takes to tackle a project like a pro. People love his innovative uses for common household items, such as plastic wrap, nonstick cooking spray, vanilla flavoring, garbage bags, fabric softener, and more. You'll find those in this book too.

"The wizard is within us all," Brian says. "We can all create our own wall magic, whether it be with paint, paper, or fabric. All it takes is a little knowledge and perception, coupled with a little more patience and persistence."

# WHAT IS COLOR?

Color is light. Scientists relate color to visible light, a band of wavelengths in the broad spectrum of electromagnetic radiation. When sunlight passes through a prism, the rays bend at different angles and the beam fans out into a rainbow of colors, ranging from red through orange, yellow, green, and blue to violet.

On a more personal level, color is how people see the world, and it's one of the ways you can personalize and organize it. Color is one of the most affordable ways available to change your home surroundings.

Effective design begins with color. It can set a room's personality, define its style, control its mood, alter its apparent size, accent its advantages, hide its faults, and turn an otherwise dull space into a warm, inviting one. A single color usually can't achieve these changes; several colors are needed to complement and reinforce a particular look or mood. This selection of colors becomes your color scheme for interior decorating.

## THE COLOR WHEEL

Interior designers usually seem to have a knack for choosing colors. Their secret? They rely on a

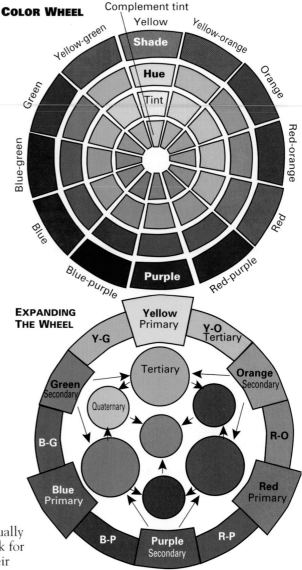

**COLOR WHEEL**

simple tool called the color wheel, which shows how colors relate to each other. Understanding these relationships and learning how colors influence each other to create different decorating schemes are easy ways to begin mastering the mysteries of color. Colors fall into different categories:

**PRIMARY COLORS:** Primary colors are the three pure colors found in sunlight—red, yellow, and blue. They are the first level of color; primaries cannot be broken into component colors and are the foundation for all other colors. Primary colors are located at equal distances around the color wheel.

**SECONDARY COLORS:** The second level of colors includes orange, green, and purple. They are called secondary colors because each is created from equal amounts of its two adjacent primary colors. On the color wheel, each secondary color falls halfway between the two primary colors it contains, and directly opposite the third primary color.

**TERTIARY COLORS:** The third level of colors includes those created by combining two secondary colors or a secondary color and a primary color, in any proportion. Purple and orange, for example, create a terra-cotta color.

Color levels build on each other. This means that you can't have secondary colors without primary colors, nor tertiary colors without secondary colors.

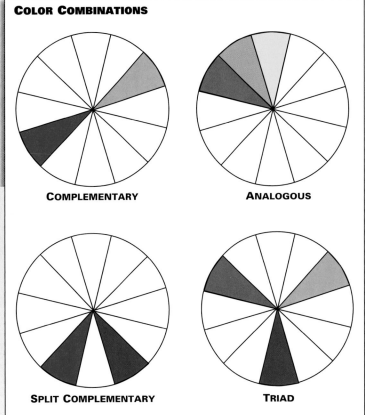

**COLOR COMBINATIONS**

COMPLEMENTARY

ANALOGOUS

SPLIT COMPLEMENTARY

TRIAD

## WALL WIZARD TIP

### COMBINING COLORS

The color wheel helps you determine which colors work well together. There are no rules about which colors should be used together, but some natural combinations are always successful. The following combinations are the easiest for beginners and those with modest experience to use in a color scheme.

■ **ANALOGOUS COLORS:** Any three colors next to each other on the color wheel. Yellow-orange, yellow, and yellow-green make an analogous arrangement. So do blue-green, blue, and blue-purple. This is a harmonious plan because the colors are closely related and your eyes easily pass over them.

■ **COMPLEMENTARY COLORS:** Colors located opposite each other on the color wheel. The best example is the red and green of Christmas. Another is peach and turquoise. By combining exact opposites, this type of color combination balances warm and cool colors. Complements stimulate one another, but can seem garish when intense colors are used. When paints of complementary colors are mixed together in equal amounts, they make a dull gray color.

■ **TRIAD COLORS:** Three colors equidistant from each other—such as red, blue, and yellow. This is a complex, lively color scheme, so controlling color values and intensities is important.

■ **SPLIT COMPLEMENTARY:** A color plus the color on each side of its complement. Pairing red with blue-green and yellow-green makes a split-complementary scheme. This subtle shift in the complementary colors enriches the scheme.

The following combinations are successful, but require a little more planning in order to be effective.

■ **DOUBLE SPLIT COMPLEMENTARY:** Four colors, one from each side of two complementary colors. This is a very rich color scheme, but difficult to do well.

■ **MONOCHROMATIC:** In this scheme, one color is used in many values and intensities so the mix stays lively and interesting. This is a sophisticated scheme that needs contrasting textures to work well.

■ **NEUTRAL:** This plan employs whites, grays, and black to build an elegant color palette. Some designers include browns—ranging from cream to chocolate— in this category. The neutral scheme requires value, intensity, and texture contrasts to be effective.

Most of these formulas require a range of values and intensities to use the colors to their best advantage. For instance, in the case of the classic red and green of Christmas, the red is a pure and intense hue while the green is deeper than the pure hue, darker in value and lower in intensity.

# QUALITIES OF COLOR

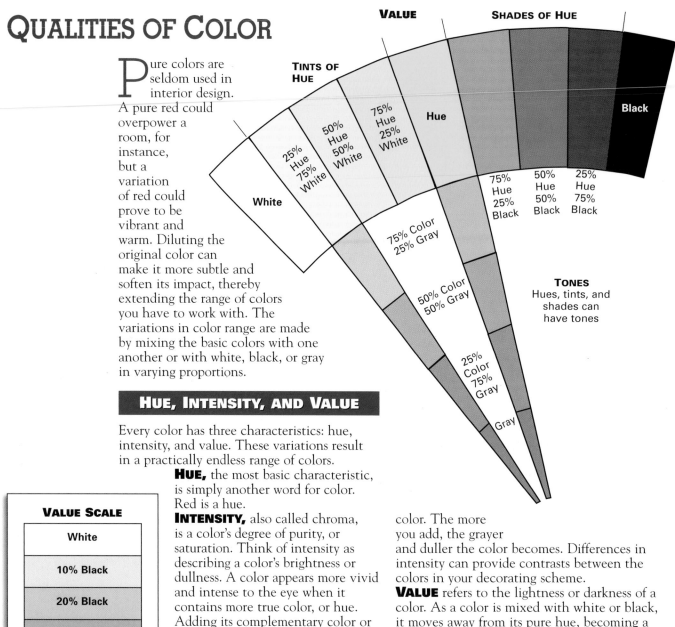

**VALUE**

**SHADES OF HUE**

**TINTS OF HUE**

25% Hue 75% White

50% Hue 50% White

75% Hue 25% White

Hue

White

Black

75% Hue 25% Black

50% Hue 50% Black

25% Hue 75% Black

75% Color 25% Gray

50% Color 50% Gray

25% Color 75% Gray

Gray

**TONES**
Hues, tints, and shades can have tones

Pure colors are seldom used in interior design. A pure red could overpower a room, for instance, but a variation of red could prove to be vibrant and warm. Diluting the original color can make it more subtle and soften its impact, thereby extending the range of colors you have to work with. The variations in color range are made by mixing the basic colors with one another or with white, black, or gray in varying proportions.

## HUE, INTENSITY, AND VALUE

Every color has three characteristics: hue, intensity, and value. These variations result in a practically endless range of colors.

**HUE,** the most basic characteristic, is simply another word for color. Red is a hue.

**INTENSITY,** also called chroma, is a color's degree of purity, or saturation. Think of intensity as describing a color's brightness or dullness. A color appears more vivid and intense to the eye when it contains more true color, or hue. Adding its complementary color or black reduces the intensity of any color. The more you add, the grayer and duller the color becomes. Differences in intensity can provide contrasts between the colors in your decorating scheme.

**VALUE** refers to the lightness or darkness of a color. As a color is mixed with white or black, it moves away from its pure hue, becoming a tint or a shade.

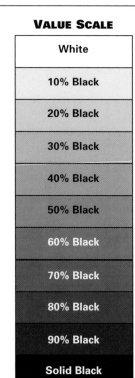

| VALUE SCALE |
| --- |
| White |
| 10% Black |
| 20% Black |
| 30% Black |
| 40% Black |
| 50% Black |
| 60% Black |
| 70% Black |
| 80% Black |
| 90% Black |
| Solid Black |

## WALL WIZARD TIP

**VALUE SCALE**

A color-value scale can help in creating a color scheme. The scale extends from white at one end to black at the other. In between are graduated shades of gray—usually shown as 10 values for convenience, although the range is continuous in nature. The shades of gray represent the relative lightness or darkness of a color—think how a color would appear in a black-and-white photograph. Pure yellow has a higher value—it's lighter— than pure blue, for instance. But you will find shades of yellow that will have the same values as tints of blue.

All colors at the same level on the scale have the same value. Bring different values of different colors into your decorating scheme to control contrast. Blue and green, for instance, don't always work well together, but a high-value pastel blue and a low-value dark green can be a pleasing combination.

A **tint** is a hue that has been lightened by adding white to it. The more white, the paler the tint. For example, pink is a tint of red.

A **shade** is a color that has been darkened by adding black. The more black, the darker the color. Forest green is a shade of green.

Mixing a color with gray gives a **tone** of the color. Mustard is a tone of yellow.

White, black, and gray—white and black mixed together—are **neutral**. Theoretically, white and black aren't colors because white reflects all the colors in the visible spectrum and black absorbs all of them. Adding neutrals to a color scheme introduces highlights and shadows, enhancing dimension.

## WALL WIZARD TIP

### COLORS WITH FEELINGS

Color often describes emotions: Red is identified with anger, green with envy, and blue with sadness. Optimists view the world through rose-colored glasses. And, of course, there's purple passion. Research has shown that colors do stimulate emotional and physical reactions in people, so each color has a psychological value that must be considered when planning a color scheme. Each color must feel right as well as look right.

### RED

Red is warm, bold, stirring, and energetic. In its pure form, it can increase a viewer's heart rate and raise body temperature. Use red in a room where activity occurs, like a family room, not one where sleeping and resting would take place. For a deep, intense setting, use other colors sparingly in a red room. The eye is drawn to red, so it makes an effective accent color.

### YELLOW AND ORANGE

Yellow and orange are just as exciting as red, but more cheerful than festive, more bright than stimulating. Yellow and orange warm and enliven any room in which they are used. They work especially well to brighten spaces and create an illusion of light in a dark room. Lighter values are best when applied to large surfaces.

### GREEN

Green is the dominant color in nature. For most people, it is pleasing, cool, fresh, calming, even restful. It is a good color for any room where you want a calm and relaxed, but fresh, atmosphere.

### BLUE

Blue—the color of sky and water—evokes fresh, cool, and restful feelings. Blue walls can make a south- or west-facing room seem cooler. Because blue recedes visually, it also lends an illusion of space and distance and feelings of haughtiness, formality, reserve, and sadness. In spite of these contradictory reactions, blue is a favorite because it is so easy on the eyes and the nerves. Blue is an excellent choice for rooms where you want to relax or sleep.

### PURPLE

Purple is lush, regal, and passionate. It is an intense and highly emotional color, partly because it straddles the line between the warm red and cool blue. This makes it a difficult color to use in interior design—it is usually used as an accent.

### BLACK AND WHITE

Black and white are pure contrasts, light and dark, all or nothing. Dramatic and elegant together, they can lend a sophistication in decorating that evokes an air of urbanity.

# DETERMINING WALL COLOR

Walls are the best places to begin designing a color scheme because they are the largest surfaces in a room. The way you finish them affects everything else you do. But the walls don't have to dominate your decorating scheme: You can decide whether the walls will provide the background for a decorating scheme or become its focal point.

**A NEUTRAL COLOR:** This makes the walls a true backdrop because they will not call attention to themselves. This is a time-proven and safe solution; it's one reason why the majority of walls are still painted white. However, white comes in more than 60 variations, each with subtle differences in tint, value, intensity, and visual warmth.

**FOCAL-POINT WALLS:** If the walls are to be the most important feature in the room as well as the largest, choose their finish first and build your color scheme around it. This is more difficult to do than picking a background color because—like an artist starting with a clean canvas—you have to decide what look you want without anything to refer to.

The easiest way to choose a color for a dominant wall is to make a selection based on your favorite colors. Another way is to decide what mood you want a room to convey. Analyze such elements as a room's function, decorative style, size, natural light, and exterior weather conditions. Then, choose a color based on those observations. Your selection should focus mainly on whether you

*Neutral walls and ceiling focus attention on the woodwork, fireplace, and Arts and Crafts furnishings in this room.*

**BACKGROUND WALLS:** Choose the color for walls that will serve as a backdrop after selecting the other major decorating elements. This lets you find a color with a balance of hue, value, and intensity that will complement all the colors in the room, in much the same way the matting around a picture emphasizes its colors. Also, thanks to modern techniques for matching and mixing custom colors, it is easy to match paint to the colors in a carpet or fabric. On the other hand, it is often impossible to find a carpet or fabric that matches an existing paint color.

The color of the wall can be a shade or tint of the room's dominant color or a shade or tint from a pattern in the room's carpet, decorative fabrics, or wallcovering. Or it can be a shade or tint drawn from a painting, an important piece of furniture, a fireplace surround, or even an outside view.

The wall color can also be a shade or tint of a color complementary to the dominant color. You probably will find the color in one of the patterned fabrics in the room. This is the best way to choose a new wall color when nothing else in the room will be changed.

*Striped wallpaper repeats colors found in the carpet and other furnishings in this young girl's bedroom.*

*Dark green walls capture attention in this solarium. The color also blends with the natural greens outside and the plants inside the room.*

want the room to be light or dark, warm or cool. If the room receives little light, the wall color should be light—unless, of course, you want the room to be dark and cozy. Whatever wall finish is used, its color, texture, and pattern should suit the room's style.

You should also consider any problems in the room when you decide on a color for rooms where the walls are the focal point. Color, texture, and pattern all can alter what you see and how you feel in a room.

In general, light colors, subtle textures, and small patterns make a room seem larger and higher, so they are ideal choices when you want the room to seem larger than it is or when you want to emphasize the spaciousness of the room. If the ceiling is too low, consider a strong vertical pattern. Dark or intense colors, bold and coarse textures, and large or busy patterns make a room seem smaller because they bring the walls close to you. That works well in a room that is too large, especially if you want a cozy, intimate effect. It can also emphasize the comfortable snugness of a small room.

For woodwork or other architectural features, decide whether you want them hidden or highlighted. To make them less visible, paint them a color that matches the wall; to make them stand out, paint them a contrasting hue.

*The walls are a main feature of this decorating scheme. Checks and stripes and exciting colors energize the walls.*

# CREATING A COLOR SCHEME

**The wall color enhances the golden glow of the sun, making this kitchen table an inviting place for breakfast.**

Designers are trained to see how colors combine with each other and how they work together. They develop an eye for color. Most designers learn this skill—they are not born with it. You, too, can develop an eye for color by studying how color is used.

Perhaps the best way to study color is to clip pictures of rooms that you like and keep them in a file. Add new clippings and color swatches as you find them. From time to time, go through them and weed out the ones that don't look as pleasing to you anymore. Over time, you'll become more aware of your likes and dislikes in colors.

Nature is a good place to start when developing a color scheme. Look at the colors in the brilliant plumage of birds or a dramatic seashore sunset. Color combinations found in nature usually please most people and are easy to recreate in your own environment.

**Dark walls give this room a dramatic high-style urban look.**

View paintings and tapestries in museums and art books. Any artwork is an excellent source of inspiration. The paintings of the Impressionists—Manet, Monet, Degas, Renoir, and others—are especially helpful because they show how areas of color merge visually to create another color when viewed from a distance.

Read decorating magazines. The articles are excellent resources because the homes shown are often created by professional interior designers. Advertisements in these magazines can be a great source of inspiration too.

Look at oriental rugs and drapery and upholstery fabrics. Study fine-quality wallcoverings, and go through some of the many wallpaper books that you can borrow from wallcovering stores.

Browse in high-quality furniture showrooms. The displays, arranged by interior designers, emphasize effective color schemes in order to sell the store's design services. Other good sources of ideas are model homes and decorator show homes.

As you research, notice how specific hues, values, and intensities are used, and what the proportions are between them. Try to relate what you see to the color wheel, and notice what combinations you find pleasing.

Don't forget to consider your own preferences. What colors make you feel happy or comfortable? You might even consider family members' complexions; you don't want to decorate your home so that everyone looks sallow. What colors dominate your wardrobe? What colors are you most often wearing when people compliment you on your appearance? These are the colors you favor naturally and that make you look your best, so they are the ideal colors for your home.

If you can't decide on colors, ask your paint dealer for color fan decks that show the color combinations available from various manufacturers.

Beware of color trends and fads. When trendsetting designers use certain colors, manufacturers begin making everything from bath towels to picture frames in these hues. Trendy colors soon become so commonplace that what once seemed new and exciting looks trite and ordinary. Then the cycle begins again with a new color. If you want to feature currently fashionable colors in your home, plan to redecorate periodically. If you want to redecorate less often, avoid trendy colors and choose those you like, whether or not they are in style. Combine them in effective color schemes for a look that you can enjoy for years.

Accent lighting washes the neutral color walls in this living room to add interest. The incandescent lights contribute warmth to the pale walls.

*The green walls in this bright and airy breakfast room look vivid in the abundant natural light.*

## LIGHTING AFFECTS COLOR

When you're considering colors for your room, look at the samples in the room itself. Lighting changes how colors look, so paint samples will look different in the store's lighting than in your home. Each type of light reflects color differently. Sunlight, which contains the wavelengths of all colors, shows the truest color. Fluorescent lighting can make a color look bluer, but some fluorescent tubes give more natural light. Incandescent lighting often strengthens reds.

Lighting fixture type and placement affect color, too. General room lighting may light walls and ceilings fairly evenly. Whether the light is natural, incandescent, or fluorescent will affect the color. Task lighting directs intense light to a specific location— usually a surface—but may leave walls unlit, making dark walls look even darker. Accent lighting adds visual interest, often by washing over walls or ceilings. Task and accent lighting may be fluorescent or incandescent.

## WALL WIZARD TECHNIQUE

### COLOR POINTERS FROM THE PRO

Here are several ways to use color with confidence.

■ If you want white walls throughout the house, use the same shade of white in every room for a unifying effect.

■ When using bright, bold colors or many different colors in a room, offset them by painting the woodwork and ceiling white. This tones down the intense colors and gives the eye a place to rest.

■ Strive for balance in the shades and tints of warm colors. A room decorated solely with pale tints looks weak and dull, overusing midtones can lead to monotony, and decorating exclusively with dark shades can make a room seem gloomy. Variety, however, will create a dynamic and refreshing decor.

■ When using different hues on the walls in each room, neutral colors in spaces between the rooms, such as hallways, will avoid clashes.

■ Pick a key color for your home and use it in some way in each room. It can be the dominant color in one room, the secondary color in another, an accent in the third, the color of an accessory in a fourth, and so on. This technique will create harmony throughout the house.

■ Light colors are expansive and airy; they make rooms appear larger and brighter. Dark colors are sophisticated and warm; they make large rooms more intimate.

■ If you want dark or intensely colored walls, seal them with a coat of clear polyurethane to enhance their depth and reflect the light. This is especially important if the room is small or dark.

■ Camouflage architectural defects with neutral paint colors that blend with neutral walls, ceiling, and floor.

■ To raise the visual height of a room, carry the wall color up to the ceiling line. If there is a crown or cove molding, paint it the same color as the wall. A light-colored ceiling also seems higher.

■ To lower a ceiling or make a room feel cozy, stop the wall color 9 to 12 inches below the ceiling and paint the band the color of the ceiling. You also can paint the ceiling a color that's darker than the walls.

■ To make a long, narrow room seem wider, paint the short walls a darker color than the long ones.

■ Coordinate a room by tinting white ceiling paint slightly with the wall color.

# PUTTING YOUR COLOR SCHEME TO WORK

Now that you know more than ever before about color, it's time to put all of that knowledge to work. Consider all of the features and furnishings of a room, from sofas, carpet, and artwork to paint and wallcoverings. When you've examined all those elements, you're ready to start developing a decorating scheme for your room or your whole house.

An effective color scheme usually combines no more than three colors, plus a neutral. Instead of adding more colors, use variations in value and intensity to create contrast between colors. The color wheel will help you choose colors that work well together. Although the colors you consider will seldom be the pure hues found on the color wheel, you should be able to estimate where they would fall on the color wheel.

## COLOR FORMULATIONS

Regardless of the color, there are only three formulations to choose from.

**STANDARD FACTORY FINISH:** This type of finish is premixed at the factory. Color selection is limited, with only popular colors available. Compared to custom-mixed colors, factory-blended paints are mixed more thoroughly, are more resistant to fading, and are more consistent.

**CUSTOM-MIXED COLORS:** These colors are mixed by retail paint dealers, decorating centers, and hardware stores. By using a light beam and a computer program, some dealers can analyze a color card or fabric swatch to determine a precise color formula. This technology makes it easy to mix virtually any color you choose.

*Red walls complement the wood floor in this dining room. The white ceiling and woodwork provide a strong contrast to the dark walls.*

## WALL WIZARD TECHNIQUE

### DESIGNER CHEAT SHEET

It's tempting to try a new paint color by simply painting a large square in the center of a wall. Professional decorators use an entirely different technique. They put the paint or wallpaper being considered on a sample board, then move the board around the room to see how the color is affected by light, pattern, and furnishings.

To make your own board, cover a 30×30-inch piece of white foamcore with the paint or wallcovering. Then hang the board on the wall in the room you are redecorating and see how it looks at different times of the day, especially at the time of day you are most likely to use the room. Move the board around so you can see how the color and pattern choices look in different parts of the room. A color that looks wonderful on the wall opposite a window may look dreadful high up in a corner or on a wall without light.

Test the board against furnishings or room features, such as floor coverings or the fireplace. Always hang the board or stand it against a wall so it will be vertical as you view it. If the color isn't right for the room, simply choose something else and start again.

*Glossy blue paint on the doors and drawer fronts introduces bright color to this white kitchen.*

**ACCENT COLORS:** Accent colors are factory-prepared pure colors, such as red, blue, yellow, or black. You mix them with one another to get rich, deep colors. Considered premium coatings, they are very durable and resist fading, so they are useful for a sunny room.

### DETERMINING THE AMOUNT OF COLOR TO USE

Your color scheme will be most effective if you use your selected colors in the right proportion. This can be difficult because few people feel confident with creating a color scheme. Most people tend to use a favorite color over and over until it loses its impact. Avoid this common mistake by developing your color scheme around one of the following models.

**ONE COLOR DOMINANT:** Use one color in its different values and intensities over most of the room. Then use complementary, analogous, triad, or split-complementary colors as accents on smaller furniture pieces, window coverings, accent rugs, and accessories such as pillows. A monochromatic arrangement is another version of this design plan. It also employs one color in shades and tints of different values. However, only one accent color is used: a contrast of the base color, often its complement.

**SPLIT COLORS:** Use one color on the walls, window coverings, and most upholstered furniture. Use a different color on the floor, and a third color along with variations of the first two for the pieces of accent furniture and accessories. This is an excellent way to use a triad or split-complementary color combination. Just be sure you get significant contrast in the colors' values and intensities.

**TWO DOMINANT COLORS:** Use one dominant color for the walls, floor, and smaller pieces of furniture, and another color for the major pieces of furniture. Because there are only two colors, pay attention to the mix of contrasting values and intensities. Add texture contrasts to the total scheme too. The textures can appear in the paint, wallcovering, or the upholstery and accessory fabrics.

*Pastels and purples enliven this child's room. The storage unit on the desk repeats the wall color on the sides and adds green and some pink.*

# THE BASICS OF PATTERN AND TEXTURE

*A large pattern stands out and attracts attention. In a small room, large patterns can be overwhelming.*

Pattern is the arrangement of the decorative design on a wallcovering. It's just as important in decorating as color. A well-designed pattern can effectively incorporate so many colors that it opens up a wide range of hues available for use in a color scheme. If chosen carefully, a design will enhance a room's colors; thoughtful contrasts in pattern can enrich the overall visual effect of a room.

## PATTERN PRINCIPLES

Pattern adds interest to a room's overall design and interacts with its decorative style. The right pattern unifies a room's color scheme and textures. Most important, it emphasizes lines, shape, and architectural features. That is why the pattern must suit the size and shape of a room as much as the decorative style. To use pattern successfully, break a pattern down into its elements and see how they fit the style of the room.

## DIMENSIONS IN PATTERN

Pattern has three attributes to consider—scale, line, and rhythm. Scale refers to the size of the design in relationship to the room and its furnishings. Strive for balance between the two so you don't overwhelm or underplay a room. A large floral print will emphasize

## WALL WIZARD TIP

### WALLPAPER PATTERNS
Wallpaper patterns fall into seven categories:

■ **LARGE PRINT:** A colorful, bold pattern that's often a realistic or stylized design based on natural forms like flowers. Large prints are best suited to large spaces.

■ **SMALL PRINT:** A pattern similar to a large print, but on a smaller scale; softer and less dominant. Works well in medium-sized and small rooms.

■ **MINI PRINT:** An arrangement of tiny design elements. Works well in small spaces and as a contrast to bold companion prints.

■ **STRIPES, CHECKS, PLAIDS, AND OTHER GEOMETRIC SHAPE:** Many geometric patterns have a contemporary feel.

■ **ABSTRACT:** Loose designs where color gives the illusion of shapes or the impression of depth. These, too, usually are contemporary in feel.

■ **TEXTURES:** Wallcoverings with a three-dimensional surface; they may be woven, like grass cloth, or embossed.

■ **BORDERS:** Narrow bands used alone on painted walls or to complement or separate wallpaper patterns

*Seen from the same distance as the large pattern on the opposite page, a medium pattern becomes less distinct and more abstract. In a large room, it can seem busy.*

*A small pattern can lend texture to walls because the pattern elements are less distinct when seen from a distance.*

the generous space in a large room and create a sense of formality. It can make an oversized room seem intimate because the walls seem closer together. However, a mini print can get lost in a large room—unless you simply want to create the appearance of texture, not pattern.

Most patterns have line, a dominant vertical or horizontal orientation. This is especially true of geometric and abstract patterns, many mini prints, and small prints like ribbons. Line should enhance a room's size and shape. For example, if a room is long and narrow or has a high ceiling, don't use a wallcovering with a strong vertical line— it will make the room seem even higher and narrower. However, if the ceiling is low, that vertical influence would make the space seem more comfortable. Random, overall patterns work best in most rooms, unless the room is so angular that the pattern will be broken up too much.

The repetition of motifs creates rhythm, the sense of movement you feel as you scan the pattern. Rhythm can create a sense of harmony in a room. If the room is for resting and relaxing, choose a pattern with a quiet or subdued rhythm. If the room is a place for physical activity, you can choose a more vigorous rhythm.

## TEXTURE

Texture adds visual interest to otherwise flat surfaces. Wood grain and marble give visual texture. Patterns printed on wallcoverings also create texture. Fabrics and some wallcoverings have visual and physical texture.

Texture on a flat surface provides light play, creating shadows and highlights. Texture serves another important need in interiors: it's a good way to disguise flaws on imperfect surfaces.

*Texture can be applied to a wall or—as in the case of this brick wall—can come from the structure of the wall itself.*

*Whether you paint a room with several bold colors like this recreation room or choose a calmer color scheme like the living room on the opposite page, latex paints make painting and cleanup easy.*

# DECORATING MATERIALS, TOOLS, AND SUPPLIES

Once you have determined your decorating scheme—which colors you'll use, which rooms you'll paint, and which ones you'll wallpaper—you can start planning your project. If you'll be doing the painting and wallpapering yourself, you'll need to buy the materials, supplies, and tools for the job and prepare the walls. This chapter will introduce you to the supplies, materials, and tools you'll need to produce a high-quality job.

# PAINT

## FOUR PARTS OF PAINT

Latex and oil-base are the two kinds of paint for home decorating projects. Each consists of four basic ingredients: solvent, binder, pigment, and additives.

**SOLVENT** (sometimes called the paint vehicle) is the liquid base of the paint and makes up the majority of the mixture. Water is the solvent for latex paints; a petrochemical solvent is the vehicle for oil-base paints.

**BINDER** holds the mixture together, helps it adhere to surfaces, and gives the surface a distinctive sheen, such as gloss.

**PIGMENT** is a finely ground powder that gives paint its color.

**ADDITIVES** in paint fulfill a variety of purposes, including reducing mildew and enhancing durability.

*Latex paint is good for walls, ceilings, and woodwork. It goes on easily and you can clean up with water.*

## THE BASIC PAINTS

**LATEX PAINT:** Latex, or water-base paint, is the most popular paint for home decorating because it dries quickly and cleans up with water. It is nonflammable, almost odor-free, and offers superior color retention when compared to oil-base paints. The binder in a high-quality latex paint is 100 percent acrylic resin. Low-quality latex paint has 100 percent vinyl resin for a binder, which decreases the durability of the paint.

A top-quality latex paint gives excellent adhesion over a variety of properly prepared surfaces, including wood, masonry, aluminum siding, and vinyl siding. Latex paints are extremely resistant to fading and cracking.

**OIL-BASE PAINT:** Oil-base paint, also called alkyd paint, was once the standard material for all painting. But do-it-yourselfers now appreciate the ease of application, low odor, and simple water cleanup of latex

paint. Oil-base paint requires mineral spirits for cleanup and contains environmentally hazardous materials. Oil-base paint is generally used for interior doors and trim today or to paint directly over existing oil-base paint. It yellows as it ages.

## VARNISHES AND STAINS

Some interior surfaces, such as trim, doors, and cabinetry, call for stain or varnish rather than paint. Instead of the opaque coating provided by paint, stains and varnishes highlight and display wood grain.

Varnish is a clear, tough coat that can be used alone on wood surfaces or applied over stained or painted surfaces. Varnish is often added as a last protective coating for woodwork. Both water-base and oil-base varnishes are available in sheens from satin to high gloss. Clear polyurethane finishes are considered varnishes.

Stain colors wood while letting the grain show through. Stain may be a dye or a pigmented product, much like thinned paint. Because stain is absorbed by the wood, it's important to add a clear finish coat for protection. Dye stains are often available in powder form to be mixed with oil, alcohol, or water. Pigmented stains are usually liquid formulations, although some are gels. Most are used directly from the can. Color-tinted clear finishes color and protect the wood, but they usually don't enhance the grain as much as a dye or pigment stain.

*A clear finish highlights the natural color and grain of the woodwork in this living room. The dark green walls provide a rich background for the wood.*

## PAINT

*continued*

*Less-reflective flat paint makes the texture of the walls less obvious in this living room.*

### SHEEN IS ALL ABOUT SHINE

Paints and varnishes are generally available in four sheens or surface lusters: flat, satin, semigloss, and gloss. Sheen—the degree of light reflectance of the paint surface—affects the finish's appearance, durability, and suitability for certain uses. The enamel value—the hardness or protective value of the coating—increases as the sheen increases.

Clear finishes are usually labeled flat, satin, semigloss, or gloss. The sheens are relatively uniform among brands.

Paint manufacturers often label different paint sheens with descriptive names, such as eggshell. Because sheens are not standardized, semigloss paint in one brand may be more or less glossy than another brand, and a third brand's satin might be glossier than either of them. Always look for sample chips that show

### WALL WIZARD TIP: PICK THE RIGHT SHEEN

| Surface | Paint | Characteristics |
|---|---|---|
| Ceiling | Flat or satin | Uniform, nonreflecting, hides flaws |
| Walls | Satin | Resists stains and has a lustrous appearance |
| Kitchen or Bathroom walls or ceiling | Semigloss Gloss | Stain-resistant and easier to clean than flat paint Durable and easy to wash |
| Kitchen cabinets | Semigloss Gloss | Stain-resistant and easier to clean than flat paint Durable and easy to wash |
| Woodwork, windows | Semigloss | Stain-resistant and easier to clean than flat paint |
| | Satin | Resists stains and has a light sheen |

surface sheen as well as color. Here are more points to consider about paint sheen.

**FLAT:** The nonreflective matte finish helps hide surface imperfections. This makes it the best choice for concealing bumps, dents and patched areas, and nail holes. Flat paint shows marks and scuffs readily, but newer scrubbable flat paints make surface cleanup easier than before.

**SATIN:** Satin paint, also called eggshell or low-luster, has a soft look, similar to the surface of an eggshell. It is more durable and mar-resistant than flat paint, and is suitable for trim, where the slight sheen helps set the trim apart from a flat-painted wall.

**SEMIGLOSS:** Semigloss paint has a higher sheen than satin paint, so it's even more mar-resistant and easier to clean. It is an excellent choice for walls and woodwork subject to heavy wear and frequent scrubbing. However, the light-reflective quality can highlight surface imperfections.

**GLOSS:** Shiny gloss paint, often labeled as gloss enamel, has the highest enamel value, which makes it the hardest, most durable type of paint. It can be a good choice for trim and cabinetry, but it really highlights surface imperfections on walls. Gloss enamel is a popular paint for kitchens and bathrooms because it's easy to clean.

*White walls, ceiling, cabinets, and woodwork make this kitchen sparkle. Gloss and semigloss paints are reflective and wipe clean easily, so the kitchen stays clean and bright looking.*

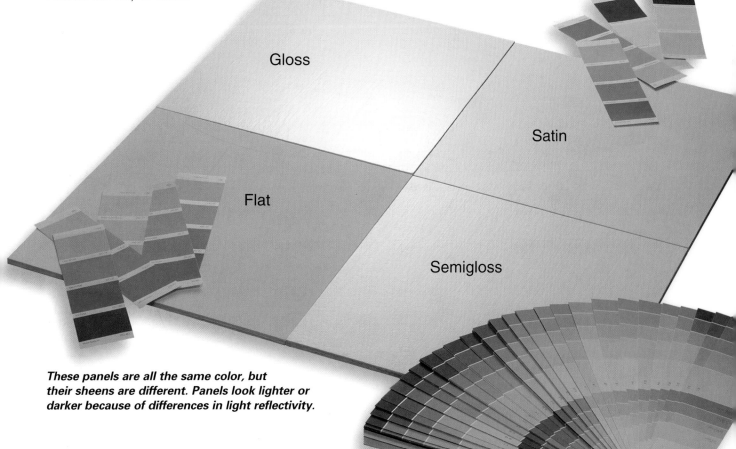

Gloss

Satin

Flat

Semigloss

*These panels are all the same color, but their sheens are different. Panels look lighter or darker because of differences in light reflectivity.*

# BUYING INTERIOR PAINTS

Always buy the best paint you can afford. Paint quality can be confusing because there are many different brands, each with its own variety of additives and enhancers. In general, there are only three grades of paint.

**LOW GRADE:** A low-grade paint is usually the lowest in price. It contains less durable binders and relies on clays and other inert ingredients to extend coverage. This type is often referred to as professional grade or architectural grade paint. It is often specified for commercial painting—in offices or apartments—where frequent repainting is standard maintenance.

**MEDIUM GRADE:** A medium-grade paint, also called decorator grade, contains many of the pigments and binders used in the maker's high-grade paint. Medium-grade paint costs slightly less than a high-grade product. This kind of paint makes an effective substitute for high-grade paint when cost is a factor. It can be a good choice when you expect to repaint every few years (for redecorating children's rooms as they grow, for example). It's also a good choice for little-used rooms, such as guest rooms, or those where there's little wear and tear.

**HIGH GRADE:** High-grade paint is the most expensive type because it contains the greatest amount of solid content of the three kinds—up to 45 percent of its contents. Compared with a low-cost interior paint, a high-grade paint spreads more easily, spatters less, and shows fewer brush marks. Also, because it contains more pigment, it hides flaws better.

In the long run, a high-grade paint can actually reduce the cost of your project because it frequently covers in only one coat. Once dry, that coat has a film that is 50 percent thicker than a coat of a low-

## WALL WIZARD TIP

### GOING WITH THE FLOW

Adding Floetrol to latex paint helps the paint bond better, stabilizes the color, lessens cracking, chipping, mold, and mildew, and can add as much as four to five years of wall life to the paint. Penetrol does the same thing for oil-base paint.

---

## *Brand Name* Interior Acrylic Latex Satin Finish

### WHERE TO USE
Most paints list the kinds of surfaces the paint can be applied over. Any limitations on use are shown here.

### COVERAGE
Paint manufacturers usually give the standard estimate of 400 square feet per gallon for coverage on painted or primed surfaces. Some labels show estimates for porous surfaces, and some tell how much you can thin the paint for spray application.

### APPLICATION
Temperature limits for application, the length of time to let the paint dry to touch, and the time needed to dry between coats are usually indicated on the label.

### INFORMATION LINE
Many paint companies have a toll-free number you can call to get answers to questions about the paint or painting.

### CARE FOR NEW PAINT
You shouldn't wash freshly painted surfaces right away. Most labels give the manufacturer's recommendation on how long to wait.

### CONTENTS
Most labels list the paint's main ingredients. The common name is usually shown along with a standard reference number that identifies the specific compound.

| CAS No. | INGREDIENT |
|---|---|
| 7732-18-5 | Water |
| unknown | Vinyl Acrylic |
| 14808-60-7 | Crystalline Silica |

Water is at the top of the list for latex paint; oil-base paint usually has alkyd as the first ingredient.

### LIMITED WARRANTY
Terms of the paint warranty are listed here. The length of the warranty coverage, the conditions and exclusions of the warranty, and how to make a claim are shown.

### CAUTION
CONTAINS CRYSTALLINE SILICA

This box contains warnings about any ingredients that may be irritating or hazardous. Precautions to take to avoid exposure and first-aid steps are shown here. An emergency medical telephone number may be given.

*Do Not Take Internally Keep Out of Reach of Children*

### *Paint Brand Name*

*Manufacturer's name and location*

*126 Fl. Oz.*

---

cost paint. The result is a tougher, more durable finish that resists fading, yellowing, staining, and abrasion. These paints are more likely to be scrubbable too.

Many paints marketed at premium prices under designers' name brands offer special surface textures or effects that can enhance a room. Linen and other fabrics, stone, and other finishes are available in special colors. Some of these paints require special preparation or tools; all call for careful application in accordance with the manufacturer's instructions to achieve the full effect. Durability varies; ask your paint dealer whether the special paint you choose will stand up to your intended use.

### READ THE LABEL

The label on a paint can tells you more than just the brand of paint. It also gives advice about using the paint and important health and safety information. Most labels include toll-free telephone numbers for obtaining product-use information and emergency medical assistance.

Signal words such as *Warning* or *Caution* indicate information about health or safety concerns you should read. Water-base latex paints, which make up about 80 percent of paint used in households, are nonflammable and have few hazards. However, some oil-base paints or special-purpose coatings could require extra caution and protection from hazards during use.

The illustration above shows some of the information to look for on a label. This example represents a label for latex paint.

*The label on the back of a paint can contains information that ranges from interesting to important. Read any health and safety warnings or cautions before you start a paint job.*

### WALL WIZARD TRICK

#### WHAT'S ON THE WALL NOW?
Always cover existing paint with the same type of paint. But how can you tell the difference between oil-base and latex? Here's one way: Scrub a small area with detergent, rinse, and towel it dry. Then rub the spot with a cotton ball soaked in ammonia. If the paint comes off, it's latex. If not, it's oil-base paint.

# BUYING INTERIOR PAINTS
*continued*

**ESTIMATING SURFACE AREA**

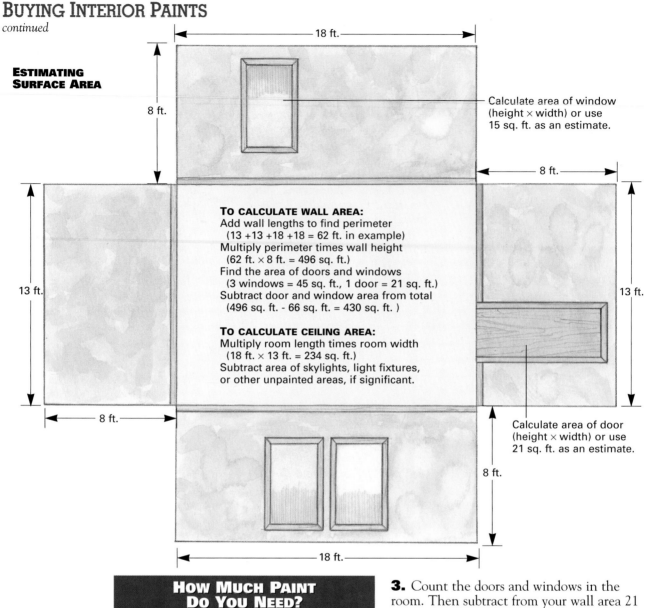

18 ft.

8 ft.

Calculate area of window (height × width) or use 15 sq. ft. as an estimate.

8 ft.

13 ft.

13 ft.

**TO CALCULATE WALL AREA:**
Add wall lengths to find perimeter
(13 +13 +18 +18 = 62 ft. in example)
Multiply perimeter times wall height
(62 ft. × 8 ft. = 496 sq. ft.)
Find the area of doors and windows
(3 windows = 45 sq. ft., 1 door = 21 sq. ft.)
Subtract door and window area from total
(496 sq. ft. - 66 sq. ft. = 430 sq. ft. )

**TO CALCULATE CEILING AREA:**
Multiply room length times room width
(18 ft. × 13 ft. = 234 sq. ft.)
Subtract area of skylights, light fixtures, or other unpainted areas, if significant.

8 ft.

Calculate area of door (height × width) or use 21 sq. ft. as an estimate.

8 ft.

18 ft.

## HOW MUCH PAINT DO YOU NEED?

There's nothing more frustrating than realizing you don't have enough paint to complete the job. And while it's good to have a little extra paint on hand for later touch-ups, it's a waste of money to be stuck with a lot of leftover paint.

To avoid either situation, accurately estimate the amount of paint you need. Here's how to make your estimate:

**1.** Begin by calculating the square footage of the surfaces to be painted. Measure the length and width of the room to determine its perimeter—the distance all around the room. For example, if the room is 13 feet wide and 18 feet long, its perimeter is 62 feet (13 feet + 13 feet + 18 feet + 18 feet).

**2.** Multiply the perimeter by the height of the room to find the number of square feet of wall area. If the room is 8 feet tall, then the wall area is 496 square feet (62 feet × 8 feet).

**3.** Count the doors and windows in the room. Then subtract from your wall area 21 square feet for each standard door and 15 square feet for each standard window. (If your room has large doors, such as a sliding patio door, or large windows, you can measure the width and height of each door and window, then figure the exact square footage of each. You don't need to be precise; round to the nearest square foot.) The room in the example has one standard door and three standard windows, so subtract 66 square feet (21 square feet + 3 × 15 square feet) from the wall area. The answer is the amount of wall area to be painted: 430 square feet (496 sq. ft. – 66 sq. ft.).

**4.** To find the number of gallons of paint needed, divide the wall area by 300—the square footage that a gallon of interior paint will easily cover. In the example, you would need a little over 1.4 gallons to paint the walls; round that up to 1½ gallons— one gallon and two quarts.

## WALL WIZARD TIP

### EARTH-FRIENDLY PAINT

Paint has become more environmentally friendly in recent years. Lead, chromium, and mercury have been removed from almost all consumer paints, and chlorofluorocarbons (CFCs) have been eliminated from aerosol paints. And manufacturers are working to reduce volatile organic compounds (VOCs), the remaining environmental concern.

VOCs are the petroleum solvents used to thin and clean up oil-base paints. Small amounts of solvent are also used in latex paints.

VOC vapors escape into the atmosphere and become part of a complex chemical reaction that produces ozone, a component of smog. At the time the problem was identified, about 2 percent of the VOCs in the atmosphere came from paint. Many of these compounds are hazardous to people and require proper personal protection.

Today, most latex paints contain no more than 10 percent solvent, and many contain only 4 to 7 percent. And solvent content of oil-base paints has dropped from 50 percent to about 20 percent.

Water-base paints have improved so much in recent years that many professional painters consider them to be better than oil-base paints. They boast greater colorfastness, better adhesion, and allow the surface to breathe better. Their easy water cleanup makes them easier to work with and releases less solvent into the environment.

*A room with a lot of woodwork and built-in storage like this bedroom will require more paint—and more time to apply it—than a room with flat walls.*

## WALL WIZARD TIP

### PAINT POINTERS

■ Although many paint manufacturers claim that one gallon of paint will cover 400 square feet, you are safer if you estimate that a gallon will cover 300 square feet of wall area. Using this figure will keep you from running out of paint before the wall is painted.

■ Always buy slightly more paint than you need to allow for spillage, waste, and spots that soak up more paint than expected. Plaster, for example, is more absorbent than wallboard. Leftover paint is handy to have for future touch-ups.

■ Buy extra paint if you plan to paint the interiors of built-in bookshelves or cabinetry.

■ Paint colors can vary slightly from batch to batch, so buy all the paint you think you'll need at one time. If you buy too little and run out, you may not be able to match the color. If your job calls for several gallons of paint, minimize color variations by mixing the cans together in a five-gallon pail. Then, pour the blended paint back into one-gallon cans.

*When you buy paint, buy extra. To keep the leftover paint in partially full cans fresh for touch-ups, exhale three times into the can to displace oxygen with carbon dioxide from your breath, then seal the can with a gasket cut from a garbage bag. Store the can upside down. (See page 71.)*

# WALLPAPER

Decorating walls by pasting paper onto them dates back hundreds of years. It still is an easy way to bring up-to-date designs into a room. Today's wallpapers are more often durable vinyl, fabric, or other materials. But the principle remains the same: Patterns and motifs that would be costly and difficult to create with paint can be applied simply and inexpensively with wallcoverings.

*The large floral pattern and pale colors give this wallpaper an old-time look.*

*The small square pattern of this wallpaper requires careful hanging to avoid a mismatched pattern or crookedness.*

*Wallpaper that matches the tile and grout colors accents the area above the cabinets and around the windows in this kitchen.*

## TYPES OF WALLCOVERINGS

Wallcoverings are available prepasted or nonpasted. Prepasted paper has factory-applied adhesive that is activated by water. This is the best do-it-yourself wallcovering. Nonpasted wallpaper has no adhesive. Paste must be applied uniformly and thoroughly when the wallcovering is installed. When you apply adhesive to nonpasted paper, you must put enough water in the adhesive to allow the wallpaper to relax and expand properly.

Various types of wallcovering have different characteristics and are suited to different uses. **ORGANIC WALLCOVERINGS**: grass cloth, cork, burlap, and anything else made with organic fibers. They may have paper backings and are best used in low-traffic areas.
**VINYL-COATED PAPERS:** a thin layer of vinyl, acrylic, or other plastic over wallpaper. This wallpaper often can be stripped or peeled and is washable. Use in low- or medium-traffic areas.
**PAPER-BACKED VINYL:** a thick layer of solid vinyl laminated to a paper backing. It's peelable, washable, and nonbreathing. Often used in bedrooms, baths, and kitchens.
**FABRIC-BACKED VINYL:** a vinyl film that is laminated to a fabric or fiberglass backing. It is durable, nonbreathing, scrubbable, and stain- and abrasion-resistant. Use in high-moisture and high-traffic areas such as laundry rooms, hallways, and stairwells.

*This embossed wallpaper adds an elegant pattern to the walls at the same time it covers cracks, holes, and other flaws. It's paintable too.*

*Organic textures, such as this grass cloth, fit into decorative schemes from casual to formal.*

*Paper-backed vinyl and solid vinyl are the best kinds of wallcoverings for moisture-prone places such as this bathroom.*

*Wallpaper is ideal for re-creating vintage decorating styles. This geometric Arts and Crafts pattern goes with the Craftsman interior.*

## WALL WIZARD TIP

### BUY MORE THAN YOU NEED
When you purchase wallcovering, both the actual square footage of material on the roll and where the design begins on the roll affect how many rolls you need. It's always better to buy more wallpaper than you need. If you run out during the job, you may not be able to find more wallcovering from the same dye lot, which might result in a noticeable color change on a wall. Stopping to buy more material delays the job too.

# WALLPAPER
*continued*

**RANDOM MATCH**

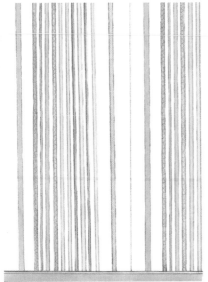

This sheet is reversed so dark shading matches sheet on left. Lighter shading then matches sheet on right, to give wider pattern.

**DROP MATCH**

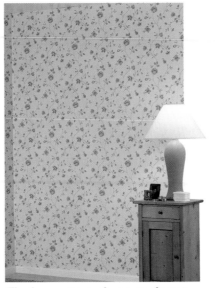

The key pattern elements do not align horizontally from one sheet to the next in a drop match. rather, the elements align on every other sheet.

**STRAIGHT ACROSS MATCH**

The key pattern elements align horizontally on all sheets in a straight across match.

## PATTERN REPEATS

The pattern repeat is the distance from one key element in the pattern to the next. The key element is the largest visual element in the pattern. Repeats range from 1 to 36 inches. The pattern repeat creates rhythm in the wallpaper's design. There are three ways to match wallcovering patterns, determined by the pattern design.

**STRAIGHT-ACROSS MATCH:** In a pattern with a straight-across match, the key element in the pattern aligns horizontally from one strip to the next.

**DROP MATCH:** With this type of match, the key pattern element aligns only every other strip. The result is a design that is broader in scale and rhythm, which in turn makes the room seem larger.

**RANDOM MATCH:** There are no patterns to match in this type of wallcovering, but there is shading to match. Random-match wallcoverings are usually natural materials or realistic representations of nonrepeating natural designs—grass cloth and textured vinyls, for example. Random-match patterns are installed using a reverse hanging method to blend the shading. In this technique, every other sheet is inverted, placing the top of the sheet at the bottom of the wall.

## WALL WIZARD TECHNIQUE: POWER GRID

We usually think of a grid as a network of intersecting lines. For wallcoverings, GRID (Greater Rhythm in Design) refers to the visual rhythm of the printed pattern. To show this rhythm best, place the pattern's key design element about 2 inches below the ceiling line (or below the molding at the top of the wall, if the room has one). If the room will have a wallpaper border at the top of the wall, place the key element so it will be below the border. This placement displays the full pattern without breaking into the key element at the top. The unbroken flow of the pattern helps hide seams too.

## USABLE YIELD OF WALLCOVERING ROLLS

| Pattern Repeat Length | Usable Yield per Roll (square feet) | |
| --- | --- | --- |
| | Euro Rolls | American Rolls |
| 0–6 inches | 25 | 32 |
| 7–12 inches | 22 | 30 |
| 13–18 inches | 20 | 27 |
| 19–23 inches | 18 | 25 |

## HOW MUCH WALLPAPER DO YOU NEED?

Wallcoverings are priced and measured by the single roll, but packaged and sold in double- or triple-roll bolts—single lengths equal to two or three rolls. To estimate the number of rolls you need, multiply the height of the wall by its length—or the perimeter of the room—then divide by 25, which is the usable square footage of a single roll. For example, an 8-foot wall 12 feet long has an area of 96 square feet. Dividing that by 25 results in 3.82 rolls of wallpaper, which rounds up to the next whole number, four. Do not deduct for standard doors and windows because you'll need the extra square footage to account for pattern repeats. If the wallpaper you choose has a pattern repeat of more than 18 inches, divide by 22 square feet instead of 25 feet.

*Covering odd angles in an attic bedroom while matching the wallpaper drop pattern may require more rolls than a quick estimate shows. Always measure carefully before buying your wallcovering.*

## QUICK ESTIMATE CHART

| Size of Room | Single Rolls of Wallcovering for Four Walls | | | | Rolls for Ceiling | Rolls of Border |
|---|---|---|---|---|---|---|
| | Height of Walls | | | | | Number of |
| | 8 feet | 9 feet | 10 feet | 12 feet | | 5-Yard Rolls |
| 8×10 | 14 | 14 | 16 | 20 | 4 | 3 |
| 10×10 | 14 | 16 | 18 | 22 | 4 | 3 |
| 10×12 | 16 | 18 | 20 | 24 | 4 | 3 |
| 10×14 | 18 | 20 | 22 | 26 | 6 | 4 |
| 12×12 | 18 | 20 | 22 | 26 | 6 | 4 |
| 12×14 | 20 | 22 | 24 | 28 | 6 | 4 |
| 12×16 | 20 | 22 | 26 | 30 | 8 | 4 |
| 12×18 | 22 | 24 | 28 | 32 | 8 | 4 |
| 12×20 | 24 | 26 | 30 | 34 | 10 | 5 |
| 14×14 | 20 | 22 | 26 | 30 | 12 | 4 |
| 14×16 | 22 | 24 | 28 | 32 | 10 | 4 |
| 14×18 | 24 | 26 | 30 | 34 | 12 | 5 |
| 14×20 | 24 | 28 | 32 | 38 | 12 | 5 |
| 14×22 | 26 | 30 | 32 | 40 | 14 | 5 |
| 16×16 | 24 | 26 | 30 | 34 | 12 | 5 |
| 16×18 | 24 | 28 | 32 | 38 | 14 | 5 |
| 16×20 | 26 | 30 | 32 | 40 | 14 | 5 |
| 16×22 | 28 | 32 | 34 | 42 | 16 | 6 |
| 16×24 | 30 | 32 | 36 | 44 | 18 | 6 |
| 18×18 | 26 | 30 | 32 | 40 | 14 | 5 |
| 18×20 | 28 | 32 | 34 | 42 | 16 | 6 |
| 18×22 | 30 | 32 | 36 | 44 | 18 | 6 |
| 18×24 | 30 | 34 | 38 | 46 | 20 | 6 |

*Find your room size in the left column, then go across to the column that shows the height of your walls. The number in that column is the number of single rolls of wallcovering required to cover four walls in the room. The number of single rolls needed for the ceiling and the number of border rolls required are shown in the right columns.*

# TOOLS FOR DECORATING

You don't need a lot of tools for a successful painting or wallpapering project, but you do need the right ones. The right tools make a project easier, faster, and much safer to complete.

For durability, buy plastic or stainless-steel painting tools. Paper products dissolve in both water-base and oil-base paints, as well as in wallpaper adhesive. And water will rust plain steel tools.

the surface better than a bargain-bin brush. A better brush usually has a sturdy hardwood handle, a nonferrous or stainless steel ferrule, and a tapered end so it makes an even line when pressed against a flat surface. A good brush has thick, flexible bristles with flagged ends. Here's how to check out a brush:

**FAN OUT THE BRISTLES:** Look for flagging—split ends on the bristles. More flagging means a brush will hold more paint.

**LIGHTLY FLEX THE BRISTLES:** They should feel springy, not limp or stiff.

**GRIP THE BRUSH BY THE HANDLE:** It should feel comfortable and not heavy; a brush that's too heavy makes your hand tired.

The kind of paint you will apply determines what kind of bristles your brush needs to have.

**FOR OIL-BASE PAINTS,** use a china bristle brush. These are natural boar's hair brushes that do not absorb oil but allow it to flow in an even, controlled manner. Clean with mineral spirits, turpentine, or acetone.

**FOR WATER-BASE PAINTS,** use a synthetic or nylon-bristle brush. Water-base paint won't stick to nylon bristles, and the nylon will not absorb water.

## PAINTBRUSHES

Always buy the best brush you can afford. A high-quality brush balances well in your hand, holds more paint, and controls paint flow onto

*The natural bristle and the nylon brushes above and above left are typical low-end brushes. A top-quality brush, such as the nylon-polyester one at left, will last longer and give better results.*

## WALL WIZARD TIP BRUSHES TO AVOID

Buy brushes for their quality, not price. A bargain brush makes painting difficult and leaves a poor-quality finish. Avoid brushes that have:

■ Coarse, black nylon bristles without flagged ends. These brushes are made to apply stripper, not paint.

■ A ferrule that isn't stainless steel or copper. Water-base paint will rust a steel ferrule; rust contaminates paint.

■ A flat, thin handle. This kind of handle is uncomfortable to hold and it's too flexible, which contributes to spattering.

### INSPECTING A BRUSH

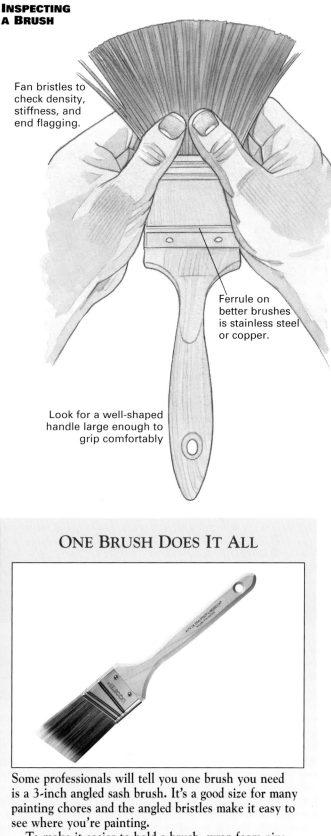

Fan bristles to check density, stiffness, and end flagging.

Ferrule on better brushes is stainless steel or copper.

Look for a well-shaped handle large enough to grip comfortably

### PARTS OF A PAINTBRUSH

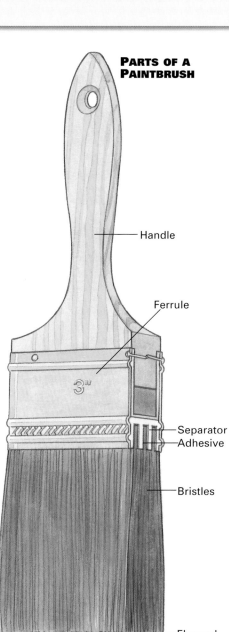

Handle

Ferrule

Separator

Adhesive

Bristles

Flagged ends

## ONE BRUSH DOES IT ALL

Some professionals will tell you one brush you need is a 3-inch angled sash brush. It's a good size for many painting chores and the angled bristles make it easy to see where you're painting.

To make it easier to hold a brush, wrap foam pipe insulation around the handle. This provides a larger and softer handle to hold, increasing control and reducing joint pain, calluses, and blisters.

## Tools for Decorating
*continued*

### PAINT PADS

The easy-to-use pad works well for cutting in, or edging, and painting flat trim. It spatters and drips less than a brush or roller. Pads can be used with either oil-base or water-base paint. Most pads come with their own paint tray and lid.

### PAINT ROLLERS

The roller ranks as the most popular applicator for do-it-yourself painters. A ½-inch foam paint roller is the best choice—it holds three to four times as much paint as a conventional roller cover. And because it does not have a nap, it won't splatter paint on you or leave fuzz in the paint on the wall.

When selecting a sponge roller or a conventional roller frame, make sure the handle is comfortable to grip and has a threaded socket in the end so you can add an extension pole. (Or buy a roller frame with a telescoping handle.) An extension handle, particularly an adjustable one, provides a fast, easy way to paint high on walls and ceilings. The long handle gives you more leverage and allows you to stand farther from the wall so you won't get as much paint spattered on you. **ROLLER COVERS:** Slip-on yellow foam roller covers designed for applying only water-base paint. Gray or blue foam covers are used only for oil-base paint. Napped roller covers must suit the surface as well as the paint type. Roller covers with shorter nap usually give a smoother finish.

**ROLLER TRAY:** If you use a metal roller tray, slide it inside a tall plastic kitchen bag, then press the bag into the pan to create a liner. The plastic keeps the paint away from metal and makes it easy to clean the tray—simply turn the bag inside out and toss it in the trash. You also can fold the plastic liner over the tray to form a lid that will keep the paint from drying during breaks.

**PAINT GRID:** A square plastic paint bucket with a built-in grid is a faster, neater way to evenly load your roller. You also can buy a separate grid to hang in your own bucket—look for a plastic one rather than metal.

### POWER APPLICATORS

Power painting tools can save time when you have large areas to cover. Two popular power painters are power rollers and paint sprayers. You can rent power-painting equipment. **POWER ROLLERS:** Once you master the technique, you'll eliminate the need to stop painting to load the roller. Power rollers let you pump paint to the roller through a hose directly from a can or a special reservoir. **PAINT SPRAYERS:** Sprayers are perfect for covering large surface areas, but they tend to use more paint than a brush or roller. They also work well on irregular surfaces such as louvered doors, panels, and wrought-iron trim. Choose a high-volume, low-pressure (HVLP) paint sprayer, which generally produces less overspray than traditional high-pressure sprayers. Preparations and masking are especially important when spray-painting.

*Spin a brush between the palms of your hands to fling out cleaning solvents. Work in an empty bucket to catch the solvents for proper disposal.*

*A mechanical brush spinner flings excess water out of a brush after cleaning. Spin the brush in a sink or an empty bucket*

Paint pads

Roller covers

Plastic roller tray

Roller extension handle

EXTENSION POLE

Roller frame

Everything that is not sealed or covered will be painted or have overspray on it, even if you use an HVLP sprayer.

## CLEANING PAINTING TOOLS

Professional painters often use the same brushes for years because they know how to care for them. Here's how to get maximum life from your brushes:

Condition new china bristle brushes by spraying the bristles with a small amount of WD40 or 3-in-1 oil. Soak synthetic-bristle brushes for latex paints in liquid fabric softener for a day, then rinse with water. These simple conditioning steps make the brush more durable and easier to clean. If you use your brushes frequently, recondition them occasionally.

Clean brushes every two hours during use and before putting them away. When dry, store each brush in its original cover or in a cardboard cover. To make a cover, measure and cut cardboard to fit around the brush, allowing for edges to overlap. Tape the edges together and slide the brush inside. Hang your brush by the handle to store it.

### CLEANING A BRUSH—LATEX PAINT:

Here's how to clean a brush that has been used for latex paint:

**1.** Scrape off excess paint against the edge of a 5-in-1 tool.

**2.** Mix a gallon of warm water with ½ cup of fabric softener in a 5-gallon bucket. Dip your brush into the mixture, swish briskly through the water, and count to 10. Your brush will be completely clean when you remove it from the water. Clean other tools in the same manner.

**3.** To dry your paintbrush quickly, use a paintbrush spinner to fling water from the brush. (Or spin the handle between the palms of your hands.) Spin the brush in a sink or an empty bucket.

### CLEANING A BRUSH—OIL-BASE PAINT:

To clean a brush used for oil-base paints, follow these steps:

**1.** Scrape off excess paint against the edge of a 5-in-1 tool.

**2.** Number three clean glass jars with lids, such as mayonnaise jars. Fill the first jar about two-thirds full with mineral spirits. Put a 50–50 mixture of mineral spirits and denatured alcohol in the second jar. Put denatured alcohol in the third jar. (See opposite page, bottom left.)

**3.** Dip the brush into jar 1, swish it around for about 10 seconds, then spin the excess out of the brush into an empty bucket.

**4.** Dip the brush into jar 2 to dissolve remaining paint, then spin.

**5.** Dip the brush in jar 3 for a final cleaning, then spin dry.

**6.** Finish by swishing the brush in a liquid fabric softener mixture as described in Step 2 of cleaning a latex-paint brush.

### CLEANING ROLLERS AND PADS:

Clean rollers the same way as described for brushes. Use the water-base method for water-base rollers and pads, and the oil-base method for oil-base rollers and pads.

Disposable roller covers are more convenient for some jobs. After the job, throw away the cover rather than clean it. To pull it off the frame, put your hand inside a plastic bag, grab the cover through the bag, pull it off, then fold the bag down over the cover for disposal. Clean the roller frame.

If you stop to take a break but will resume painting later, wrap the roller cover tightly with plastic food wrap instead of cleaning it. The wrap will keep the paint from drying on the roller.

*Compact HVLP sprayers and power paint rollers are ideal for interior painting.*

WAGNER HVLP

WAGNER 949 POWER ROLLER

# SETUP AND CLEANUP TOOLS

Common tools that will come in handy during a decorating project include an electric drill (corded or cordless), vacuum cleaner (a shop vacuum is best), safety goggles, cap or hat, tape measure, apron, hammer, screwdrivers, broom and dustpan, and dusting brush.

Lay a piece of plywood or a flush wooden door over two sawhorses for a work table. Set up your table in another room, or outside if you will be using solvents for oil-base paints.

Keep a 5-gallon bucket of water, a tile sponge (this kind holds more water), and some dry towels handy throughout the job. Here are more tools and materials that will make preparation and cleanup easier.

**3-IN-1 PAINT OPENER:** This is the proper tool for opening a paint can, but it's hard to find. A key-shaped paint-can opener is a good substitute.

**BLUE MASKING TAPE:** Also called painter's tape, this tape is tacky enough to stick but does not pull off the paint. To avoid seepage, run a flat plastic edge across the tape to seal. Use this in place of beige masking tape, which can damage the surface.

**PAINTER'S PRETAPED MASKING FILM:** This handy combination of blue masking tape and plastic sheeting creates an instant drop cloth with tape along one edge. It comes in a cartridge that fits into a container with a cutting edge. The film protects the 24 inches from the wall where most accidents

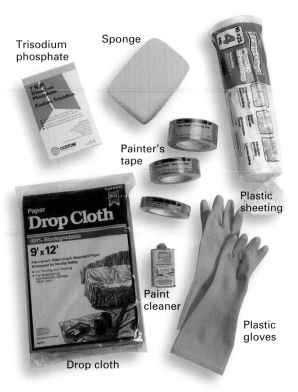

Trisodium phosphate

Sponge

Painter's tape

Plastic sheeting

Paper **Drop Cloth** 100% Biodegradable 9'x12'

Paint cleaner

Plastic gloves

Drop cloth

occur. The plastic clings to the surface and paint that drops on it dries almost instantly. It's biodegradable, too.

**PLASTIC GLOVES:** Use plastic gloves; latex gloves tear easily and are porous, allowing paint to come through.

**DROP CLOTHS:** The best drop cloths have a heavy plastic side and a paper side. Always lay it so the absorbent paper side is up. Never use newsprint for drop cloths; the black ink can mar clean surfaces. Bedsheets are too porous.

**PLASTIC SHEETING:** Filmy $\frac{1}{2}$-mil sheeting works fine to cover walls when stripping wallpaper. Cover floors and large furniture with heavier 4-mil material.

**SPONGE MOP WITH SCRUBBING HEAD:** A scrubbing sponge on the head makes scrubbing the walls a cinch with this mop.

**ROLLING MOP BUCKET:** You don't have to bend over or have a hand free to move this bucket on wheels—you just push it along with your foot, it minimizes back strain.

**TRISODIUM PHOSPHATE:** Known as TSP, this agent washes off dirt and grime and deglosses surfaces. Mix $\frac{1}{4}$ cup with a gallon of warm water to wash walls. Apply it to the walls with the sponge mop, let it set for two or three minutes, then scrub the walls with an abrasive pad—called wet sanding.

6 inches

First cut

6 inches

1 inch

Second cut

Third cut

1 inch

## WALL WIZARD TRICK

### APRON IS BAGGY, BUT NOT TRASHY

A garbage bag makes a fine apron to keep paint off your clothes. To make an apron, hold a 13-gallon tall kitchen plastic trash bag with the open end down. Fold it in half lengthwise. Opposite the folded edge, cut off the top corner in an arcing cut to make the arm holes. Cut the neck hole, starting at the folded side about 1 inch below the top edge. Leave shoulder straps about 1 inch wide between the neck hole and the arm holes. You can slit the sides of the apron for more roominess.

Wear eye protection and plastic gloves—TSP is caustic.

**PAINT CLEANER:** A water-soluble, citrus-based cleaner removes paint from rugs, floors, and woodwork.

**NONSTICK KITCHEN SPRAY:** Kitchen vegetable spray will keep paint from sticking to your skin. Apply it to exposed skin before you start painting.

**VINEGAR:** Stir 1 cup of vinegar into 1 gallon of water to rinse walls.

**PLASTIC FOOD WRAP:** Clingy plastic food wrap protects anything that can't be removed from a room, including doorknobs, knockers, and ceramic towel racks. Wrap the telephone receiver to protect it from messy hands. Pull a sheet taut over the front of your glasses to protect them from spatters.

**CORNSTARCH OR BABY POWDER:** Before putting on plastic or rubber gloves, sprinkle your hands with either of these to keep them from getting sweaty and wet.

**BABY WIPES:** These are good for easy cleanup. They are safer than combustible oil-soaked rags.

## LADDERS

Professional painters use a variety of ladders, including a 5-foot platform ladder, a four-segment multifunction ladder, and a 10-foot extension ladder.

For everyday jobs, choose a 5-foot platform ladder. A platform ladder is usually made of aluminum and features a top step designed to stand on. A platform ladder allows you to face a wall you are working on. For ease of use, buy one that you can open and close with one hand. For safety, apply nonskid strips to each step. The legs should have nonskid tips. You can often rent specialty ladders or scaffolds for large decorating jobs.

## WALL WIZARD TRICK

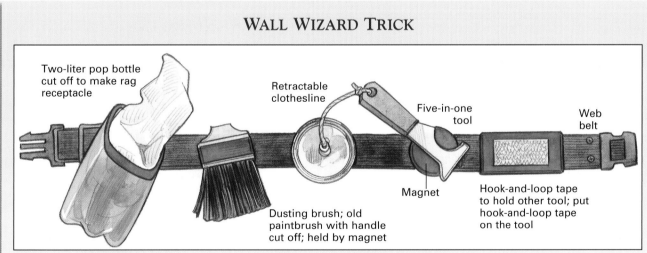

Two-liter pop bottle cut off to make rag receptacle

Retractable clothesline

Five-in-one tool

Web belt

Dusting brush; old paintbrush with handle cut off; held by magnet

Magnet

Hook-and-loop tape to hold other tool; put hook-and-loop tape on the tool

### MAKING A PAINTER'S BELT

You'll save time if you have your tools with you at all times. An easy-to-make painter's belt will keep your tools within reach. Start with a snap-on web belt, available from home centers and hardware stores.

■ Fasten a pot magnet to the belt with a machine screw, nut, and two fender washers. The magnet will hold a dusting brush with a steel ferrule, a broad knife with a tempered steel blade, or other tools.

■ Cut the top off a plastic soda bottle to make a cup to hold rags and baby wipes. Cut two slits in the back so it will slide onto the belt.

■ Bolt a retractable lingerie clothesline to the belt and attach your 5-in-1 tool or other tool to the line. Attach another pot magnet next to the reel to hold the tool.

■ Apply the hook side of a self-adhesive hook-and-loop tape to the belt. Attach the loop side to any tools you want to keep on your belt.

■ If the belt seems too heavy to wear around your waist, add suspenders for support. You can hang more tools on the suspenders.

# PREPARATION TOOLS

Preparing your walls is an important part of a painting or wallpapering job. Here are some tools and supplies you'll need:

**PAINTER'S BUDDY:** Also called a 5-in-1 tool, this handy item has a point for digging out old caulking or opening cracks on plaster, a scraper head for removing wallpaper and old paint, a spackle edge for laying spackle or filling holes, and a curved edge for cleaning paint from a roller. The hard end of the handle drives popped screws and nails back into the wall. It's small enough to fit in a back pocket or on your tool belt.

**CAULKING MATERIALS:** Caulking packaged in an aerosol can is handy for filling gaps between woodwork and walls. You'll need a caulking gun and a tube of caulk to fill larger gaps and cracks. Twist a large wire nut onto the spout to keep caulk from oozing out between uses.

**PATCHING MATERIALS:** Spackle, wallboard joint compound, or patching plaster will fill holes and cracks in the walls. Home centers and hardware stores sell a number of ready-to-use patching compounds in handy dispensers; pick the ones that fit your needs. You'll also need sandpaper, drywall sanding screen, and a sanding block to do a smooth patching job.

Wallpaper perforator

Scraper

5-in-1 tool

Broad knife

Plastic garden sprayer

Spackling compound

Caulking gun and caulk

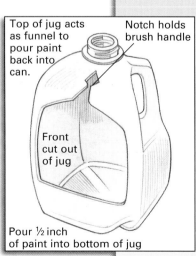
**BROAD KNIFE:** Used for patching, a broad knife has a wide, flat edge that's ideal for smoothing patching compound. A 6-inch flexible broad knife, a 2-inch putty knife, and paint scrapers, both hooked and straight, will prove useful during preparation.

**GARDEN SPRAYER:** A pump-up plastic garden sprayer quickly applies wallpaper remover to large areas. Buy a new sprayer; don't use one that has been used for herbicides or pesticides.

**PERFORATING TOOL:** If you have to remove wallpaper, this tool, called a Paper Tiger, will save you time. Roll it over the wallpaper to perforate the surface so wallpaper remover can get to the adhesive.

**BROOM HANDLE:** Use a broom handle to roll strippable wallcoverings off the wall and to prevent the drywall's paper surface from tearing during removal.

## WALLPAPERING TOOLS

You'll need some additional tools for hanging wallpaper.

**PLUMB LINE:** A plumb line is the best way to establish a vertical line on the wall. Don't use a level to draw a plumb line. Place a push pin at the top of the wall and let the line and weight dangle. When the weight stops swinging, the line is plumb. Snap it to mark a chalk line on the wall. Use yellow chalk; blue will show through wallpaper and paint.

**WALLPAPER-SMOOTHING BRUSH:** A plastic wallpaper-smoothing brush will smooth wallpaper and eliminate air pockets without squeezing out adhesive. The brush is usually 12 inches wide with 3-inch bristles.

**6-INCH AND 1-INCH METAL BROAD KNIFE:** Use a broad knife as a guide to score and trim wallpaper with a knife. The broad knife protects your hands from the knife blade. Don't smooth the wallcovering with a broad knife—it can tear the material and squeeze out adhesive. Use a smoothing brush.

**PLASTIC SQUEEGEE:** Set seams with a squeegee rather than a seam roller. You can exert enough force with the roller to force all the adhesive out of the seam.

**SNAP-OFF KNIFE:** Made with a plastic handle and replaceable metal snap-off blades, this type of knife gives you a fresh, sharp tip each time you cut wallpaper.

**PLASTIC GARDEN PLANTER BOX:** A planter box holds water to activate the adhesive on wallpaper rolls—just don't get one that has drainage holes in the bottom. Boxes made for wetting wallpaper are also available at home centers and decorating stores— but you probably won't need an expensive, high-quality one for home use.

Water tray

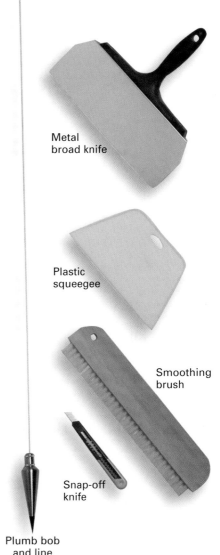

Metal broad knife

Plastic squeegee

Smoothing brush

Snap-off knife

Plumb bob and line

## WALL WIZARD TRICK

### STEP UP ON PAINT-BUCKET STILTS

To reach up to paint trim and hang wallpaper borders more easily, strap these stilts to your feet. You'll need two 5-gallon paint buckets with lids. Put your shoe on the lid, and mark the lid for hook-and-loop straps at the toe and heel. Attach double-sided hook-and-loop material to the lids with machine screws, fender washers, and nuts. Put two strips at the heel to wrap around your ankles. Glue a rubber pad to the bottom of each bucket to prevent slipping. Move slowly.

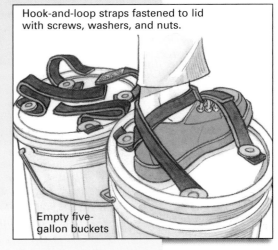

Hook-and-loop straps fastened to lid with screws, washers, and nuts.

Empty five-gallon buckets

# PREPARATION

About 80 percent of the work done by any professional painter or wallpaper hanger is preparation—not installation. Care taken during this important first stage gives a high-quality look to the finished project. All room surfaces should be prepped—scrubbed, repaired, and smoothed—before they are painted or wallpapered. You'll probably put in one to three hours of prep time for every hour you spend painting or wallpapering. This chapter shows you how to prepare for redecorating correctly and easily.

**Most of the work in painting or wallpapering involves preparation. Filling nail holes is one of the steps toward a perfect paint job.**

# CLEAR THE ROOM

The easiest room to paint or wallpaper is an empty one. Move everything out of the room, then thoroughly vacuum or mop the floor and wipe the baseboards and woodwork clean. Cover the floor with plastic sheeting, and fasten the edges to the floor with duct tape. Lay cloth tarps over the plastic.

If you can't move everything out of a room, move out what you can, then gather as much of the rest as you can in the middle of the room. Start by moving the large furniture to one side of the room. Clean the floor and baseboards on the clear side, cover the floor, then repeat for the other side of the room. Place the furniture and accessories in the center of the room. Cover everything with plastic sheeting, then with drop cloths, to protect from spatters.

Turn off the power to any outlets or fixtures on the surfaces you will be painting or wallpapering. Remove all light fixtures, switch and outlet plates, heat registers, towel rods—anything that you would have to paint

### MARK THE HARDWARE HOLES
After removing drapery hardware and other fixtures, poke toothpicks into the holes. This makes it easy to find the hole for reinstallation. When reattaching the hardware, snap off the exposed toothpicks, leaving the rest of the toothpick inside so the screws will bite securely into the wall.

around. Tag each item with its location and keep screws and mounting hardware with it to make reinstallation easier. Pay particular attention to how your window treatments are attached. Draw a diagram or make notes if necessary, then put them in a plastic bag with the hardware. As you remove small items, put them into plastic bags and label the bags by room. Tape the bags to a windowpane with masking tape—this keeps the bags off the floor and prevents the small parts from getting lost or broken.

*Clearing the room before you start makes it easier to prepare the walls and ceiling and apply the paint. Move as much furniture as possible to another room and cover the rest.*

In some cases, you can loosen the canopy of a ceiling fixture or chandelier—the trim piece right against the ceiling. Then you can slide the canopy down the fixture away from the ceiling while the fixture remains solidly in place. You can then cover the fixture with plastic lawn bags. Never unscrew a fixture from the electrical box and allow it to hang just by its wires. It is usually better to remove a fan. Cover outlets and switches with duct tape to shield them from paint and moisture.

Make cleanup easier by lining a bucket with several plastic garbage bags. As you work, fill the bag with scraps and trash, removing each bag when it gets full. When the job is done, toss the drop cloths, disposable brushes, steel wool, and all other debris onto the plastic sheeting on the floor and roll it into a ball for easy disposal.

*Plastic sheeting protects this furniture from paint drips and spatters. Don't use old bedsheets; paint passes right through the porous fabric.*

## WALL WIZARD TIP

### DO THE JOB SAFELY
Taking steps before painting or wallpapering can protect you from potential hazards.

### SAFETY RULES TO FOLLOW:
■ Shut off the power at the circuit breaker to the room you are painting or wallpapering.
■ Follow the manufacturer's instructions and safety precautions for all products.
■ Keep pets and children out of work areas.
■ Keep all paint and wallpaper products out of the reach of children.
■ Wear safety glasses or goggles when working overhead, using strong chemicals that may splash, or creating or cleaning up dust. Wearing a full face shield is a good idea when working overhead or with solvents.
■ Rub vegetable spray or oil onto your hands, arms, and neck before working. Wash as quickly as possible after working.
■ Open doors and windows when you are working with solvents. Use an exhaust fan, as well, if the air is still and humid.

■ Turn off all sources of flame—including appliance pilot lights—when spraying any compound or paint that contains a solvent.
■ Use wet baby wipes instead of cotton rags to help prevent spontaneous combustion.
■ Secure all scaffold planks. Extend the plank 1 foot beyond a support at each end and clamp or nail it into place. Do not step on the plank between its support and its end.
■ Check the manufacturer's label on your ladder to make sure that it can support your weight plus the weight of the tools or materials you will carry up it.
■ Keep the area clear by dropping debris into a plastic-lined bucket or trash can as you work.
■ Create a secure storage area where you can keep tools—especially sharp ones—and materials not in use.
■ Keep solvents away from flame or fire, and don't smoke near them.
■ Don't work with solvent-based chemicals if you are pregnant or have heart or lung problems.

■ Rinse oil- or solvent-soaked rags and spread them out to dry—don't wad them up. Dispose of them carefully. If you want to reuse rags, launder them thoroughly and spread them out to air-dry.
■ Open the legs of a stepladder fully, lock the leg braces, and make sure the ladder sits level and steady on the floor.
■ Never stand on the top step of a stepladder, its braces, or work shelf.
■ Step down and move the ladder instead of stretching to reach farther.
■ Position an extension ladder so the distance between its feet and the wall it leans against is one-fourth of the ladder's height. Most extension ladders have a sticker on the side showing the proper leaning angle.
■ Follow the manufacturer's instructions when you operate power painting equipment.
■ Do not apply cleaning agents or wallpaper remover with the same garden sprayer you use for garden chemicals.

# CLEANING, CAULKING, AND SANDING

After covering the floor, removing fixtures, and protecting the furnishings in a room, it's time to clean the walls. Cleaning helps paint and wallpaper adhere. The wall should dry for a day before painting or wallpapering. Cleaning walls is easier when one person scrubs and another rinses.

First, remove the greasy film that forms on all walls. Dust the surfaces with a vacuum cleaner or sweep them with a clean broom or dust mop. Then, wash the walls with a low-phosphate multipurpose household cleaner mixed according to the manufacturer's instructions. To make your own solution, combine a gallon of warm water with ¼ cup trisodium phosphate (TSP), or a substitute, in a 5-gallon bucket. Mix well.

Using a sponge mop with a scrubbing head, wash the wall from the bottom up with the sponge side, working around the room. When you reach your starting point, turn the mop head around and begin scrubbing the wall. This technique is called wet sanding. If you plan to paint the ceiling, wash it first. Change the cleaning solution often to keep it clean.

For rinsing, mix 1 cup of white vinegar in a gallon of lukewarm water. Vinegar, an astringent, neutralizes phosphors that might prevent the paint or wallpaper from bonding to the wall. Apply the rinse to the wall with a clean sponge mop; use a fresh gallon of rinse for each wall.

## TACKLING TOUGH STAINS

**MILDEW:** Spots that look like splotches of dirt on your walls might be mold and mildew. These fungi thrive in warm, damp rooms with poor ventilation. To test the spot, dab a small amount of household bleach onto it. If the spot comes off, it's mold or mildew.

To remove mold or mildew, mix 1 teaspoon of dishwashing detergent and 2 cups of hydrogen peroxide into 1 gallon of warm water. Wear gloves and goggles. Apply the solution with a sponge or mop and let stand for several minutes. Several applications may be needed. Rinse with a solution of 1 cup of vinegar in 1 gallon of water. When dry, lightly sand the places where the mildew appeared. To seal against recurrence, apply two coats of white-pigmented, oil-base sealer; sand between coats.

**GREASE-BASED STAINS:** Stubborn grease stains require an additional cleaning step. To remove the stain, rub it with a liquid deglosser such as Oops! or Goof Off to break the oil film. When dry, sand the area with 120-grit paper, then wipe away the sanding dust. Seal with two coats of white-pigmented, oil-base sealer; sand between coats.

**RUST AND WATER STAINS:** Rust and water stains will show through new paint. To remove them, scrub with a solution of 2 tablespoons of TSP in 1 cup of warm water. Rinse with a mixture of 1 cup vinegar in 1 gallon of warm water. Allow to dry for several days, then sand with 120-grit paper. Seal with two coats of white-pigmented, oil-base sealer; sand between coats.

**MARKER AND CRAYON STAINS:** Fold an old T-shirt into a pad several layers thick and place it over a crayon mark, then set an iron at medium heat and run it over the pad. For permanent markers, lightly dab the spot with nail polish remover. Rub the spot with a liquid deglosser. When dry, sand with 120-grit paper, then wipe away the sanding dust. Seal with two coats of white-pigmented, oil-base sealer; sand between coats.

**PANELING ADHESIVE:** To remove paneling adhesive, scrape or chisel off as much as possible. Lightly sand, then apply two coats of oil-base sealer. Spackle the surface, then seal again.

*A coat of paint is flexible and thinner than a piece of paper. Flaws in the surface under the paint will show and stains can bleed through the new paint, so careful preparation is the secret behind making old walls and woodwork look this good.*

## CLEANING CEILINGS

Clean a painted, nontextured drywall or plaster ceiling just as you would a painted wall. Smooth or lightly textured ceiling tile can be cleaned with a sponge mop too.

If the ceiling has a sprayed-on texture coating, first determine if it has been painted before. If it is unpainted, don't wash it; wetting the texture could damage it. Spray on an oil-base sealer to prepare the ceiling for painting.

You can wash a previously painted ceiling. Mix 1 cup of vinegar and 2 tablespoons of baking soda in 1 gallon of water, and spray the solution on with a garden sprayer.

## CLEANING MASONRY WALLS

Before cleaning any masonry surface, scrub it with a nylon-bristle brush and TSP. Remove any alkali deposits with a mixture of muriatic acid and water. Wearing full-length rubber gloves and goggles, pour 1 cup of muriatic acid into 3 quarts of water. (Always add acid to water, never the other way around. Neutralize spilled acid with baking soda.) Scrub the surface with the acid solution and a brush. Rinse with water, and let dry.
**SEALING:** Coat the wall with penetrating sealer as soon as possible after the acid solution dries. Masonry surface conditioner, sold by paint dealers, seals and hardens unpainted masonry as well as masonry covered with aging paint. If the surface has flaking paint, scrub it off with TSP and a scrub brush, then rinse with a solution of 1 cup of vinegar in 1 gallon of water.

## CAULKING

Caulking is important for painting and wallpapering. It fills in all gaps along baseboards, moldings, and trim, and provides a cushion so wallpaper can be more easily trimmed. Apply caulk with a caulking gun according to manufacturer's instructions. A white, water-based acrylic caulk works best. After you have applied caulking to a surface, blend the bead into the moldings with a slightly dampened sponge. Allow the caulk to dry overnight.

## SANDING

Sanding is the key to a flawless finish. In most cases, light dry-sanding will be enough to polish the surface. (If you have holes or cracks to patch in the wall, do that first, then sand to ensure a smooth surface.) A wallboard sanding screen, a hand-sanding block, or a power sander will do the job. For power

sanding, a palm sander or half-sheet orbital sander works best; belt sanders abrade the surface too much. Sand drywall and plaster along the longest direction; sand wood with the grain.

You don't need to dry-sand walls and ceilings with flat or semigloss paint that have been wet sanded with a low-phosphate cleaner. High-gloss paints should be lightly sanded with 150-grit sandpaper. Wipe off dust with a tack cloth and change sandpaper frequently. Wear a respirator; close off the room to keep dust from spreading. Place a box fan in the window, front side facing out, to remove fine dust from the room.

*A random orbital palm sander does a great job on woodwork and also can sand walls quickly and easily.*

*A flexible contour sander works well on curved moldings.*

# REPAIRING SURFACES

**PATCHING WITH REINFORCING TAPE**

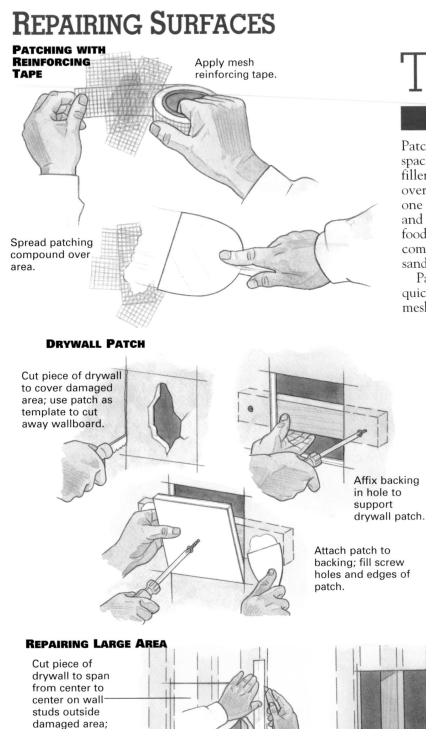

Apply mesh reinforcing tape.

Spread patching compound over area.

**DRYWALL PATCH**

Cut piece of drywall to cover damaged area; use patch as template to cut away wallboard.

Affix backing in hole to support drywall patch.

Attach patch to backing; fill screw holes and edges of patch.

**REPAIRING LARGE AREA**

Cut piece of drywall to span from center to center on wall studs outside damaged area; use patch as template to cut away wallboard.

Attach patch to studs; fill screw holes and edges of patch.

To get professional-looking painting and wallpapering results, start with a smooth, blemish-free surface. Here's how:

## PATCHING HOLES

Patch small holes in drywall or plaster with spackle or drywall joint compound. Press the filler into the hole with a broad knife; don't overfill. Several thin coats are better than one thick one. When working on white walls and molding, mix one or two drops of red food coloring into every 6 ounces of patching compound to make it easy to spot repairs for sanding later.

Patch medium-sized holes in walls with a quick-drying plaster compound. Put fiberglass-mesh reinforcing tape over the hole, then apply the filler and let it dry. Sand, then apply a top coat of drywall compound and sand it smooth after it dries.

Secure a patch for a large hole to backing strips or wall studs. Here's how to patch a large hole:

**1.** Measure the hole. Cut a piece of drywall large enough to cover it. Trace around the patch onto the wall, and with a drywall saw, cut out the marked area. If the patch is large enough to extend from one stud to another, cut the opening to the center of each stud so you'll have nailing surfaces for the patch.

**2.** Cut one or more backer strips out of plywood, 1× boards, or drywall scraps. They should be 3 to 4 inches wider than the hole. Slip them behind the opening and secure them to the wall with 1-inch wallboard screws.

**3.** Lightly coat the edges of the hole and the patch with joint compound. Push the patch into the opening and fasten it to the backer strips with drywall screws. If the ends lay on studs, fasten the patch to the studs.

**4.** Apply strips of self-adhesive fiberglass mesh tape or paper joint tape to the seams, overlapping the tape at the ends.

**5.** Work a coat of joint compound into and over the tape. Apply the compound horizontally, then smooth it vertically. This is called the crisscross technique. Let dry overnight. Sand with 120-grit sandpaper.

**6.** Skim a second coat of compound over the entire patch. Let dry completely.

**7.** Sand with 120-grit sandpaper; apply two coats of white-pigmented, oil-base sealer.

## REPAIRING WOODWORK

Patch small holes, such as nail holes, in wood trim with a wood-filling compound. If the woodwork in the room is clear-finished rather than painted, fill any holes and defects with a matching wood filler or stainable latex wood putty, and let dry. Where woodwork has extensive damage, it is usually easier to replace the moldings, unless they are antique or custom trim that cannot be readily matched. In that case, you should consult a professional finish carpenter.

Sand the patched areas with 150-grit sandpaper. Then lightly sand the entire surface. Vacuum, then wipe the woodwork with a tack cloth to pick up dust.

Stain the patched areas for trim that will receive a clear finish. After staining, apply two thin coats of clear finish.

## REPAIRING DRYWALL

Drywall can develop cracks, especially at joints and corners. Popped nails, holes, and open joints are common problems.

**REPAIRING POPPED NAILS:** Normal expansion and contraction of a house can cause some wallboard nails to pop out over time. Fix them with this four-step method.

**1.** Drive a 1¼-inch wallboard screw into the stud or joist, about 2 inches from the popped nail, to pull the wallboard tight against the framing. Recess the head slightly.

**2.** Drive the popped nail into the wallboard.

**3.** With a 6-inch broad knife, cover the nail and screw heads with lightweight spackle. Let dry overnight; lightly wet-sand. Apply a thin second coat. Let dry overnight.

**4.** Apply two coats of white-pigmented sealer to the porous spackle patches to keep the paint sheen consistent. The sealer also promotes proper adhesion for paint and wallpaper and keeps any color variations from showing through the paint.

**FILLING OPEN JOINTS:** Stress-point cracks are hard to repair because they can reappear when the house shifts. The secret to filling such cracks is to use an interior vinyl spackling paste. It will remain flexible and

will expand and contract as the house shifts.

**1.** If the crack is more than a hairline fissure but narrower than ¼ inch, widen it slightly and undercut its sides with a linoleum knife. Whatever its size, vacuum, sponge, or brush out the crack to remove all loose debris.

**2.** Apply interior vinyl spackling with a 6-inch broad knife, using the crisscrossing technique. Let dry overnight.

**3.** Sand with 120-grit sandpaper.

**4.** Reinforce the patched joint along its entire length with self-adhesive fiberglass mesh or moistened paper joint tape. Apply more of the spackling compound over the tape with a 6-inch broad knife, using the crisscross technique. Let the patch dry. If necessary, sand again and apply a third coat with a wider knife.

**5.** Wet-sand the patch and allow to dry.

**6.** Seal the repair with two coats of white-pigmented sealer.

### REPAIRING A CRACK

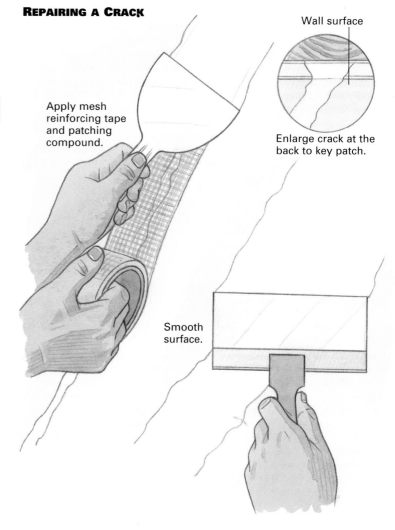

Apply mesh reinforcing tape and patching compound.

Wall surface

Enlarge crack at the back to key patch.

Smooth surface.

# REPAIRING SURFACES
*continued*

## REPAIRING HOLES IN PLASTER

Support damaged area with plaster screws.

Dampen edges before patching.

Apply patching plaster in two coats.

## REPAIRING PLASTER

For lath-and-plaster walls, extensive damage or areas larger than 12 inches square should be repaired by a professional plasterer. Repair cracks by cleaning out the crack with a linoleum knife, then filling it with spackling compound. Sand smooth.

### REPAIRING A CRACK

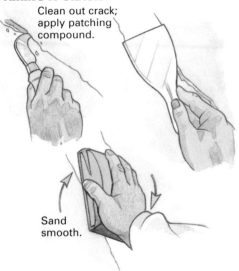

Clean out crack; apply patching compound.

Sand smooth.

### REINFORCING LOOSE PLASTER:

When plaster is sound but sagging away from the underlying lath, repair it by screwing it to the lath with 1½-inch wallboard screws and plaster washers (available at home centers).

**1.** Thread the washer onto the screw. Drive the screw through the plaster into the lath, using a power drill-driver. Drive the screw in until the washer is drawn into the plaster surface. Space the screws 4 inches apart, and drive them into studs or joists if possible.

**2.** Cover the washers with spackling compound. Let dry.

**3.** Sand the area with 120-grit sandpaper. Sand the patches flush with the wall.

**4.** Seal the repaired area with white-pigmented shellac.

### REPAIRING HOLES:

Remove all loose and damaged material back to a sound edge. If the plaster around the damaged area is loose, reinforce it with screws. If the lath is damaged in the repair area, place metal lath or other reinforcing material over the broken lath in the hole.

**1.** Remove loose material with a putty knife or chisel. Dust the area with a clean brush. Add a drop of dishwashing detergent

### PLASTER SCREWS

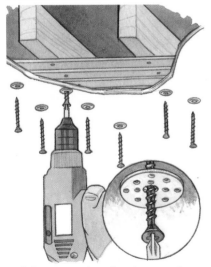

Drive screws into framing members if possible.

to a bucket of water, and dampen the edges of the plaster. You can also use a commercial latex bonding agent; mix and apply it according to the manufacturer's instructions.

**2.** Mix patching plaster, following the manufacturer's instructions.

**3.** Apply the plaster with a broadknife. If the hole is less than ¼ inch deep, one coat should be enough.

If the hole is deeper than ¼ inch, apply a base coat of plaster in the hole to within ¼ inch of the surface. Press the plaster into the lath. Let this coat set for 15 minutes, then score the surface with a nail to provide tooth for the next layer. Let the base dry overnight.

**4.** Apply a second layer of patching plaster, bringing it almost to the surface. Let this layer set for an hour.

**5.** Add water to bring the patching plaster to a creamy consistency for the finish coat. Apply the finish coat, making it as smooth as possible. Make the patched area flush with the surrounding surface. Let the finish coat set for 30 minutes to an hour.

**6.** Smooth the patch with a damp sponge, blending it into the surrounding surface. This will reduce the amount of sanding necessary. Let the plaster harden.

**7.** Seal the area with white-pigmented shellac.

## REPAIRING MASONRY

Latex masonry paints are thick enough to fill small flaws such as hairline cracks. To repair larger flaws in brick and concrete block walls, dig out any loose material and dust the crack or hole with a clean brush. Then wet the area and patch with cement or mortar. Wet the repaired area and let it cure for two weeks.

# SMOOTHING SURFACES

You can paint textured surfaces if they're clean and sound, but wallpaper requires a smooth surface. Here's how to remove texture.

**TEXTURED WALLS:** Sanding stucco, plaster, or textured paint from a wall is a dirty, difficult job. Instead, cover over—or float—the textured surface with joint compound. Also called mudding, this technique is quick, inexpensive, and fairly easy to do. It will take parts of three days. Be sure to wear a respirator when scraping and sanding. You can float any surface using this same method.

**1.** Prepare the room and clean the walls.

**2.** Lightly sand the entire wall with a pole sander to knock down any roughness or high peaks on the wall. Do not scrape textured surfaces.

**3.** Dust the walls with a clean broom or vacuum cleaner.

**4.** Spot-seal any damaged areas with two coats of white-pigmented, oil-base sealer. Use a disposable brush or a roller with a disposable cover. Let the spots dry. Sand lightly with a 120-grit sanding screen.

**5.** Thin premixed joint compound with water in a 5-gallon bucket until it is the consistency of thick yogurt. A drill with a propeller-type mixer blade is the best tool for this.

**6.** Divide each surface into 4-foot-square sections. Scoop the compound into a drywall tray.

**7.** Apply the compound to the 4×4-foot sections with large, sweeping strokes.

To float a wall, start in a bottom corner. Apply the joint compound to the first 4×4-foot section with a 10-inch broad knife. It's usually easiest for right-handers to work from right to left. Repeat on each adjoining section until the lower half of the wall is covered. Return to the starting edge of the wall and float the top half of the wall in the same way. Let the compound dry overnight.

Lightly sand the wall, then apply another thin layer of compound for a smooth surface. Apply oil-base sealer after wet-sanding.

**PANELING:** Wallpapering or painting directly over paneling is not recommended. Cover the paneling with special liner paper—a kind of wallpaper—or install ¼-inch drywall over the paneling.

**TEXTURED CEILINGS:** Sprayed-on ceiling texture could contain asbestos. (See page 51.) If you are not sure whether it does, assume it has asbestos until a test proves otherwise. There are two ways to smooth a ceiling:

■ Cover the ceiling with drywall, as

**PREPARING A WALL FOR FLOATING**

Lightly sand to remove peaks and roughness.

Apply sealer to damaged areas.

explained below in "Installing New Drywall."

■ Remove nonasbestos texturing by soaking it with a solution of 1 cup of ammonia and 1 cup of fabric softener in 1 gallon of water. Let the solution soak in for about 15 minutes then scrape the texture off with a floor squeegee. Cover the floor well with taped-down plastic; this is messy.

## INSTALLING NEW DRYWALL

The most time- and cost-effective way to smooth a large surface is often to install new drywall over it. Place ¼- or ⅜-inch-thick sheets of drywall vertically against the wall or lengthwise on a ceiling, then attach them with screws driven into the studs or joists. You can install a plastic vapor barrier over the old wall before you install the new drywall. Of course, you must remove all woodwork before hanging the drywall and reinstall it afterward. Tape and finish the drywall joints.

**FLOATING A WALL**

Work in sections, starting at bottom of wall.

# REMOVING OLD PAINT

A chemical paint stripper is a good choice for removing paint from old moldings. Once the stripper has softened the paint, scrape it off. Multiple coats may require several applications.

This sponge-tipped tube fills a nail hole with spackle and neatly smooths it in one step. It's one of many handy painting preparation aids available at paint stores and home centers.

## REMOVING OLD PAINT FROM WOODWORK

You can paint or install wallpaper over old, sound paint on walls. For best results on woodwork, strip off chipped paint or finish. Strip down to bare wood if the existing finish is layered thickly, if large areas are damaged, or if you are going to change to a different finish (from oil-base to latex, for instance). The appropriate stripping method depends on the size and number of chipped spots and the type of finish you will apply. Whenever you remove old paint by any method, wear safety goggles, plastic gloves, long sleeves, and a dust mask or respirator.

**DRY SCRAPING:** Scrape off old paint with a 6-inch broad knife. Scrape loose paint and debris until you reach a firm surface. Lightly sand the surface with 120-grit sandpaper.

**CHEMICAL STRIPPING:** A chemical paint remover is the best choice when removing a finish down to bare wood.

Paint-stripping chemicals are highly caustic. Wear protective gear, including safety goggles, a respirator, plastic apron, knee pads, and latex gloves. Professional painters first put on a pair of surgical gloves, wet their gloved hands with water or rub on a coat of petroleum jelly, then slip on a pair of latex gloves. This establishes a strong barrier against the caustic chemical. Follow the paint remover manufacturer's directions for use, and always work in a well-ventilated area.

When removing paint with a chemical stripper, follow these steps:

**1.** Work in 1-foot-square sections. Use a disposable brush. Brush a thick coat of the stripper in one direction over the painted surface. Do not brush back and forth—this will reduce the chemical's effectiveness. Let the stripper stand for the recommended time, plus 10 minutes, allowing the paint to soften so it can be easily removed. Apply another coat if the first one dries out.

**2.** Scrape away as much of the softened paint as possible with a coarse abrasive pad, a putty knife, or a nylon pot scrubber. Clean the abrasive pad when it becomes clogged. Use paint thinner to clean oil-base strippers and water for water-base strippers.

**3.** Rub the cleaned surface with a fine abrasive pad and denatured alcohol to remove the last bits of paint and neutralize the surface. Rub with the grain of the wood. Let dry for at least 24 hours.

**HEAT:** Softening paint with an electric heat gun is not generally recommended because it is tedious, potentially hazardous, and less

effective than chemical paint removers. Also, it leaves paint embedded in the wood grain, which you have to remove with a chemical stripper. If you do use a heat gun, wear heavy leather work gloves, a respirator, and goggles. Follow the manufacturer's instructions for how long and how close to hold the gun to the surface. Take care not to scorch the wood or set the paint on fire. Never use a heat gun on a surface that has been treated with a chemical stripper or to remove paint that contains lead.

*Old wallpaper has been stripped from this stairwell. Next comes the important step of removing all traces of wallpaper adhesive (see pages 52–54).*

## HAZARDS IN THE HOME: LEAD AND ASBESTOS

Lead and asbestos are hazardous materials that demand special attention. Any home built before 1970 probably has materials in it that contain asbestos. And paint that was applied as recently as 1978 could contain lead. In some cases, you'll need to call a professional contractor to stabilize or remove these materials.

### LEAD
The older the paint, the more likely it contains lead. Almost all paint once contained lead, but with the development of latex paints, lead content declined from the 1950s until lead limits were set for all paints in 1978. Dust and chips from damaged or degraded lead paint can contaminate your house and cause serious health problems for you and your family. For safety, lead-bearing paint in your home that's loose, chipped, or breaking down should be abated.

The best ways to abate lead-paint hazards in a house include:
■ Paint removal. Scrape paint from peeling walls and woodwork with a broad knife. Wear a respirator as you work. You can apply chemical paint strippers to soften the paint. If you

dry-scrape the paint, mist the surface with a spray bottle as you work to reduce hazardous dust. Clean up dust and particles with a wet mop—a vacuum cleaner will spread lead dust into the air.

Sanding, sandblasting, and similar methods aren't recommended because of the dust hazard. And softening lead paint with a heat gun could create toxic fumes.
■ Encapsulation. Instead of removing the paint, isolate it or seal it off. Apply new drywall over the existing wall or float the wall with wallboard compound, as described on page 49.
■ Surface replacement. Remove and replace woodwork and moldings painted with lead paint.

### ASBESTOS
Asbestos has been linked to a number of serious lung diseases. Any home built before 1970 probably contains building materials made with asbestos—anything from sheet flooring to textured ceiling sprays. If these materials are in good, sound condition, they probably aren't a threat. Asbestos-containing

*An easy-to-use swab, available from home centers and paint stores, tests for lead in paint. The end turns pink when rubbed over paint that contains lead.*

material becomes a problem when it is damaged or disturbed, releasing asbestos fibers into the air.

You can cover an asbestos-containing surface, such as a textured ceiling, with new wallboard or float it with wallboard compound. Don't try to scrape the texture material off. If you want to remove it—or any material containing asbestos, hire an asbestos abatement contractor to take it off and dispose of it safely.

# REMOVING OLD WALLPAPER

If you are painting or wallpapering a room that is already wallpapered, you will probably have to remove the old wallpaper. Always remove old wallpaper before hanging new because the old wallpaper may not be adhered well and it could come loose from the wall when the new wallpaper wets it. Also colors in the old paper might bleed through new wallpaper or paint. Wallpaper textures and seams will show through new paint. Paint and new wallpaper will not adhere to some kinds of wallpaper, such as foils.

## PAINTING OVER WALLPAPER

Professionals usually recommend removing old wallpaper instead of painting over it. Painting over wallpaper is a quick fix, but removing it will yield a better paint job and will save you from having to remove painted wallpaper in the future.

If you do decide to paint over wallpaper, make sure the wallcovering is firmly bonded to the wall. Using 150-grit open mesh sanding screen, dry-sand the surface, smoothing any irregularities and roughing up the surface so the paint will stick. Dust the surface with a large broom. Apply two thin coats of sealer or oil-base undercoater to the wall. When dry, paint the wall.

## REMOVING WALLPAPER

When removing old wallpaper, be sure to remove all traces of the old paste from the walls too. Paint will crackle when applied over wallpaper paste and new wallpaper won't adhere well over it. Here are the four ways to remove wallpaper:

**DRY REMOVAL:** The easiest way to remove wallpaper is to pull it off the wall—but that isn't always possible. You can simply peel off strippable vinyl wallcovering that has a solid vinyl or fabric backing if the walls were properly prepared and the wallcovering was hung correctly. Try dry removal first. Working from the top, pull about 2 inches of the wallcovering loose from the wall for the full width of a strip. Wrap it around a broom handle or 1-inch dowel, then carefully roll the dowel down the wall, wrapping the wallpaper around it. Rolling it off this way is easier because the even pressure on the wallpaper prevents it from tearing as much. It also reduces damage to the drywall surface. When the wallpaper is off, remove adhesive from the wall using the wet removal method (below). The iodine test (see the opposite page) will show where adhesive remains.

**WET REMOVAL:** This effective but messy method will remove any kind of wallpaper from any wall surface, even multiple layers or painted-over wallpaper. It also removes paste from the wall after dry removal. Turn off power to the room. Tape plastic to the floor and cover anything else in the vicinity that shouldn't get wet.

**1.** Go over the wallcovering with a special perforating tool—usually called a Paper Tiger. The tool's rotary teeth poke holes through the surface of the wallcovering, allowing the water to reach the adhesive behind the paper. Attack the wall with two Paper Tigers—one in each hand—to save time. Start at the top left corner of the wall and work down and across the wall, making large circles. Poke about 10 holes per square inch.

**DRY WALLPAPER REMOVAL**

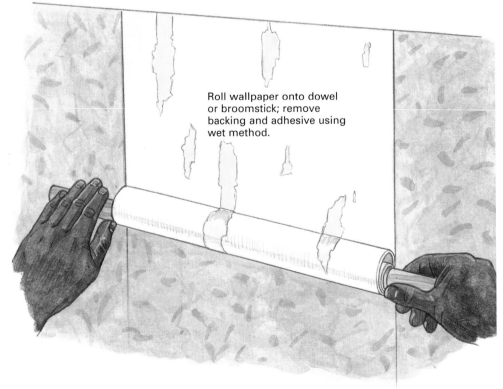

Roll wallpaper onto dowel or broomstick; remove backing and adhesive using wet method.

**2.** In a plastic 5-gallon bucket, mix a solution of 3 gallons of hot water, 22 ounces wallpaper remover concentrate containing enzymes, ¼ cup liquid fabric softener, 1 cup white vinegar, and 2 tablespoons baking soda. The solution remains active for about 15 minutes after you mix it.

**3.** Pour the mixture into a plastic garden sprayer and adjust the nozzle for a medium mist. (Spray on the remover with a new garden sprayer or one that has not been used to apply garden chemicals.) Spray the walls from the bottom up, working from left to right. Go around the room three times. Move quickly (or work on just one wall at a time) to stay within the 15-minute active time for the solution. Change to a fresh solution often to ensure that the chemical reaction is working.

**4.** When the walls are saturated, place ½-mil plastic sheeting over them, smoothing it in place with a wallpaper brush. Make sure the

### REMOVING STUBBORN SPOTS

Scrape off, holding scraper at low angle to avoid damage to wall.

Wet with wallpaper removal solution.

### WET WALLPAPER REMOVAL

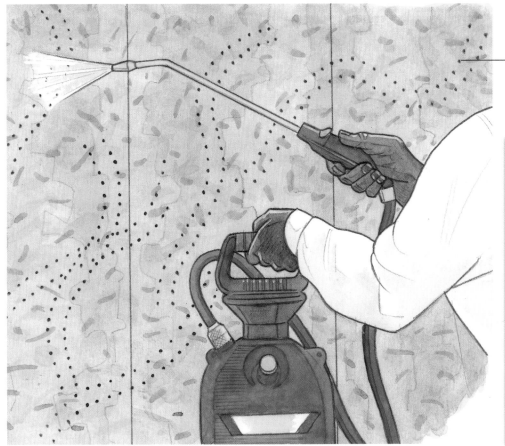

Perforate wallpaper with rotary perforating tool.

Spray remover solution on wall with plastic garden sprayer.

### WALL WIZARD TRICK

#### IODINE TEST
The iodine test will make old adhesive on walls visible by turning it brown or purple. If you don't remove all old adhesive, paint will crackle over it and wallpaper won't stick. Simply mix 1 ounce of iodine with a quart of water and pour into a trigger pump spray bottle. Spray sparingly; iodine stains.

plastic is tight and smooth, with no air bubbles. Have another person assist you during this process. Leave the plastic on the wall for at least three hours. It can stay overnight.

**5.** Test to determine whether the adhesive has released. Pull back a lower corner of the plastic, then gently scrape the wallpaper from a corner with a broadknife to see if it is loose enough for removal. If it resists, carefully pull the plastic away from the wall in small areas and spray more solution onto the wallpaper. Replace the plastic and let the remover work for an additional six to 12 hours.

**6.** To remove the paper, take off the plastic to uncover an area as wide as two wallpaper strips. Pull the plastic straight down (not out) from the top. Using a broad knife, carefully lift and remove the wallpaper. Work from the top down, left to right. Hold the scraper or wallpaper removal tool at a low angle so you don't gouge the damp wall. Spray the removal solution on stubborn spots. When all of the wallpaper has been removed, conduct the iodine test to make sure the walls are free of old adhesive.

**GEL REMOVAL:** Wallpaper removers are available in gel form too. The advantage of gel remover over wet stripping is that it sticks to the wall better than the watery solution. It's not as effective in removing entire pieces of wallpaper or multiple layers, however. Gel removers are useful for removing borders. To use the gel, first perforate the surface as described in the wet removal instructions on pages 52–53. Apply the gel according to the manufacturer's instructions.

**STEAM REMOVAL:** Professionals often use steam to strip off wallpaper. Steam removal is not recommended for do-it-yourselfers, though. Steaming can damage drywall if done incorrectly. If you do use a steam wallpaper remover, follow the manufacturer's instructions precisely and ask the rental store or dealer for operating advice.

## CLEAN THE WALL

After you have stripped several sections, wash the wall to remove any last traces of adhesive. Clean carefully where seams were, along baseboards, and along door and window trim—places where adhesive might have built up. The easiest way to wash the wall is with a sponge-head floor mop. The long handle lets you reach from floor to ceiling, and the sponge soaks up water and rinses easily. Scrub the wall from top down with clear, lukewarm water. Rinse the mop often, and change the water in the mop bucket when it becomes cloudy so you don't smear adhesive all over the wall. Dry the wall with old towels. Repair the wall if necessary (see pages 46–48). Wait 24 hours before painting or installing wallpaper.

**MASKING WINDOWS**

Tape along edges of glass.

Mask edge of casing.

Spread lip balm along edge of glass to mask it.

### WALL WIZARD TIP

**WALLPAPER REMOVER**
Wallcovering adhesives are starch-based; the enzymes in wallpaper remover work by eating the starch to weaken the bond. Perforating the wallpaper allows the remover to get directly to the adhesive. Keeping the remover wet by trapping it under plastic keeps the solution working.

# FINAL STEPS IN PREPARATION

With wall and woodwork cleaning and repair completed, the last thing to do before painting is to mask and drape the room. You need to cover any exposed surfaces that won't be painted to protect them from spatters, drips, and spills.

If you are wallpapering, masking usually isn't needed. Make sure the joints between the walls and moldings and trim are tight or caulked so you can trim the wallcovering to the moldings accurately. If the trim and moldings will be painted, do it before hanging the new wallcovering.

## MASKING WOODWORK

Masking protects your woodwork—whether bare or finished—from splotches and spatters as you paint the walls.

**1.** Use 2-inch-wide blue masking tape; seal the edge by running a plastic spatula or the end of your knife handle along it. Apply tape along the side edge of window and door trims. The stuck edge should abut the wall. Leave the outside edge loose. Remove masking tape within 15 minutes after painting.

**2.** If your project includes painting windows, mask the glazing. Tape along the edges of the glass or spread lip balm on it to mask next to the molding. After painting, you can easily remove lip balm by heating it with a hairdryer and buffing the glass with a dry cotton rag.

## DRAPING WALLS

If you are painting the ceiling, drape the walls to protect them and the woodwork from spatters and drips.

**1.** Press the top half of 2-inch-wide blue masking tape along the top of the walls. Butt the top edge of the tape against the ceiling to make a neat joint line. You can use pretaped masking film for draping too.

**2.** Push plastic sheeting under the loose lower edge of the tape and press the tape down onto the plastic. Let the sheeting drape down over the walls and baseboards.

**3.** About an hour after painting, remove the tape and sheeting.

## SETTING UP THE WORKSPACE FOR WALLPAPERING

Set up a cutting and pasting table outside the room you are wallpapering. If nearby, the garage or patio makes a good location because spilled water will do less damage. If you set up a table in an adjoining room, spread plastic

**DRAPING WALLS**

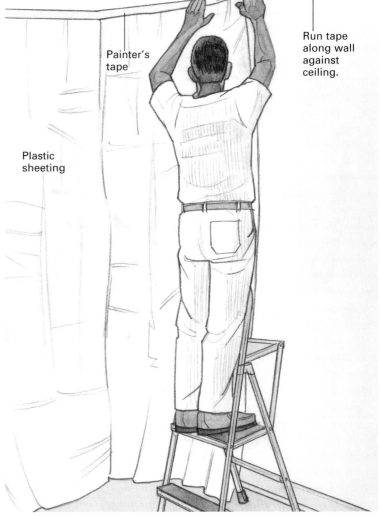

Painter's tape

Run tape along wall against ceiling.

Plastic sheeting

on the floor beneath it. To make the table, lay a 4×8-foot piece of ¾-inch plywood or a 36-inch-wide hollow core door over sawhorses. Never cut wallpaper on the floor; the paper will get dirty. Working at table height makes cutting easier too.

### WALL WIZARD TIP

**TOOTHPASTE IS FOR TEETH**
Some people like to fill little holes in walls with toothpaste. You're better off using spackle or some other material intended for patching walls rather than giving you a sparkling smile. Toothpaste doesn't hold up over time and color sparkles or bleaches can show through the paint.

*Basic brush and roller techniques are all you need to know, even when painting a room with an elaborate multicolor— often called polychrome— scheme like this.*

*Following the basic painting instructions in this chapter will help you give your home a paint job that's just as smooth, even, and flawless as the one in this room.*

# BASIC PAINTING
# TECHNIQUES

Anyone can master the painting skills to apply a beautiful, durable paint job. In this chapter you will learn about priming and sealing surfaces for painting and how to prepare the paint for application. Then you will find out about techniques for painting walls, ceilings, and trim, including some professional painters' tricks and tips that will help you do the job quickly and easily.

Once you've completed the patching and preparation, painting goes quickly. You can paint a room in a few hours with a brush and a roller.

# PRIMING AND SEALING

Applying sealer, primer, or sizing to a surface will improve the appearance and durability of the finish.

Sealer, also called undercoater, includes white-pigmented sealers, oil-base undercoaters, and sanding sealers. Applied over a porous surface, sealer prevents absorption of later coats and provides an even base for them. Sealer is often applied to isolate surface problems—such as discoloration, knots in wood, or mildew— to keep them from bleeding through and marring the new finish.

Some sealers are available in spray cans that offer good coverage and easy application. An inexpensive trigger handle for the spray can makes the spray can easier to control and eliminates painted fingers and hand cramps.

Primer prepares a surface for wallcovering. Primer provides a uniform base color and gives the surface tooth for better adhesion. Primers are generally acrylic, water-base products, so they dry faster than paint.

Sizing is a thin adhesive applied to plaster to make it ready for wallpapering. Primer is often used in place of wall sizing. Sizing should not be applied under paint.

## WALL WIZARD TIP: PRIMER OR SEALER?

### WHEN TO USE A SEALER

Apply a sealer before painting porous surfaces such as these:

■ Any unpainted surface, including new plaster, drywall, and old woodwork that has been stripped.

■ Large areas of wallboard joint compound or patching plaster.

■ Masonry surfaces such as unglazed brick, cinder block, or concrete.

■ Bare open-grained wood, such as oak.

■ Bare woods, such as redwood or cedar, that bleed through or discolor paint.

■ Metal surfaces; use oil-base primer-sealer with rust inhibitors to prevent corrosion.

■ Over dark or bright colors that you want to cover with lighter paint.

### WHEN TO USE A PRIMER

Apply primer when installing wallcoverings on nonporous surfaces such as these:

■ Any surface painted with a glossy finish.

■ Existing paint that is sound, but worn.

■ Painted wallboard or plaster.

# GET THE PAINT READY FOR THE JOB

Buy all the paint you'll need for a room at one time. Ask the dealer to shake the paint on a mixing machine. If you start work within a week after bringing home machine-shaken paint, a light stirring is all it needs. When you open a paint can, punch small holes into the bottom of the groove around the rim (the lid well) to let paint that gets into the well drain back into the can. Put the can lid in a plastic bag to keep the paint on it from drying.

If paint has been sitting for a week or longer, take it to the paint dealer for shaking. If you can't get it shaken, an electric drill with a propeller-type paint mixer is the best way to stir a single can that has been sitting for a while. Poke the mixer shaft through a paper plate, then hold the plate against the open top of the can to prevent paint spattering as you run the drill.

## BOXING

If you have several cans for the job, the color could vary slightly among the cans. To ensure a uniform color throughout your job, mix all the paint together, called boxing.

Pour all the paint for the job into a plastic 5-gallon pail. Stir it thoroughly with a stick until it is mixed and uniform in color. Pour the boxed paint back into the cans. Tightly seal the lids on all but the first can.

## STRAINING

Straining eliminates lumps in the paint. New paint (less than a year old) usually doesn't need straining. If the paint has separated, stir the thick paint up from the bottom of each can until it is as free of lumps as possible. Then box the paint, pouring it through a nylon paint strainer into the pail.

If the paint has a thick scum or skin, remove the skin and set it aside. When the skin has dried, wrap it in newspaper and discard it. Box the paint, pouring it through a nylon paint strainer into the pail.

## CONDITIONER

Paint that has been stored for a year or longer may need conditioner to improve its flow, adhesion, and coverage. (Paint that's more than three years old is probably no good.) Stir the paint, then add a conditioner such as Floetrol to water-base paint, following the manufacturer's instructions. You can add conditioner to new paint too. It retards drying, making it easier to maintain a wet edge as you paint—important for reducing overlap marks. Penetrol is a conditioner for oil-base paint. If you have stirred and conditioned the paint but it does not flow or adhere properly, ask your paint dealer about it. You may be using the wrong brush or roller, or your surface may not be prepared properly.

## THREE LAWS OF PAINTING

■ Paint from a plastic pail, not the can. Professional painters always paint from a bucket. Keep the paint in a sealed can so it stays fresh. The brush can carry contaminants from the surface into the paint; using a pail keeps unused paint from being contaminated. An open paint can is easy to spill too, especially the gallon size.

■ Pour no more than $\frac{1}{2}$ inch of paint into a tray or bucket. This forces you to refresh the paint often, making it flow, stick, and cover better. It's less weight to carry around, too, and if you do spill, there's less to clean up.

■ Air dries paint. While working, minimize exposure of your paint supply to air. Paint left in open containers will thicken, then dry. Paint will dry in uncleaned tools and brushes left in the air.

---

### WALL WIZARD TIP

#### PAINT DABS SHOW COLOR

Dab paint on the outside of the can to show the color. Also, brush a patch of paint inside a switch plate in the painted room and write the color name or number on it. You can take the plate along with you for matching other decorating elements later.

---

### WALL WIZARD TRICK

#### TAPE ON A PAINT BUCKET

To hold paint without fatigue, tape a 2-quart plastic bucket to your hand with duct tape. Set the bucket on the palm of the hand you don't brush with. Wrap a strip of duct tape down one side of the bucket, around your hand, and up the other side. Taping the bucket to your hand is much less tiring than gripping the bucket's wire handle. Place a strong bar magnet on the outside of the bucket and one on the inside—they hold each other in place—and hang your brush on the one inside the bucket.

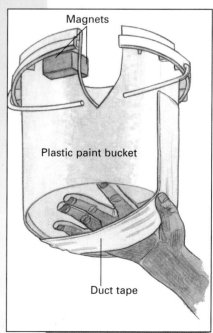

Magnets

Plastic paint bucket

Duct tape

# PAINTING TECHNIQUES

Painting skills are not difficult to learn. Most of them come naturally, but knowing some of the techniques professional painters use can help you do your project quickly and easily and give results you'll be proud of.

## PAINTING WITH A BRUSH

You can paint any surface, from walls to trim, with a brush. Brushes are suited to painting woodwork, cabinets, and smooth-textured surfaces. A brush is ideal for cutting in wall and ceiling corners and edges, too, because it spreads paint efficiently and gives you more control. Use an angled sash brush to paint window sashes and to cut in edges (see page 63). A brush about 3 to 4 inches wide is usually a good choice for interior painting. Don't paint with the edge of a brush; that splays the bristles and distorts their shape.

## HOLDING A PAINTBRUSH

There are three good ways to hold a brush.
■ Grip the brush lightly, with your thumb underneath and your fingers on top of the ferrule. Let the handle rest in the joint where your thumb joins your hand.
■ Hold a small trim brush like a pen or pencil, with the handle resting in the hollow of your thumb joint.
■ Wrap your hand around the handle with your thumb on top. This grip is good if your hand is small or you are painting with a large brush. To minimize fatigue, shift your grip from time to time.

For comfort, slip a 6- to 8-inch length of foam pipe insulation over the handle. This doubles the diameter of the handle and pads it, which can reduce joint and tendon pain.

## LOADING A BRUSH

To load your brush, remember these three steps: dip, wiggle, and pat.
■ Dip the bristles straight into the paint, no deeper than one-third of the bristle length.
■ Wiggle the brush in the paint.
■ Pat the brush lightly against the inside of the pail as you lift it out. This is better than scraping the brush across the rim. Scraping can break and damage the bristles.

## BRUSHING PAINT

Start at the left bottom corner of a wall and paint from the bottom up with strokes about 16 to 18 inches long. Apply the paint in three strokes for a smooth finish:
■ Unload the brush or pad with the first upward stroke.
■ Set the paint with a gentle stroke downward over the first.
■ Smooth the paint with a gentle upward stroke to remove brush marks. Keep the end and edge of the stroke wet to prevent overlap lines from developing between strokes.

Continue moving up and along the wall using this technique. When you have painted from the bottom of the wall to the top, make one continuous, final upward stroke to eliminate overlap lines and brush marks.

**THREE WAYS TO HOLD A PAINTBRUSH**

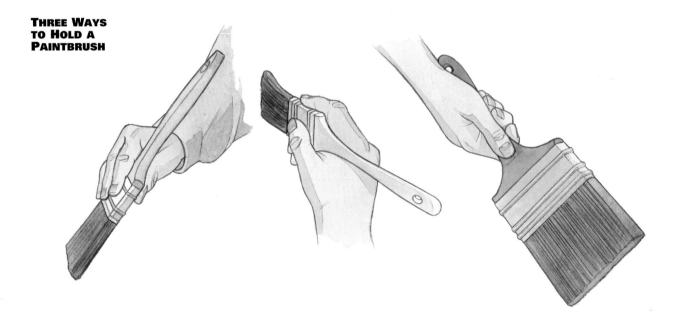

## PAINTING WITH A ROLLER

Rollers spread paint so quickly and easily that they have become the preferred tool for painting large, flat surfaces. Start by slightly moistening the roller cover with water for latex paint or paint thinner for oil-base paint. After dampening the cover, dry it with a clean towel. Dampening and drying removes lint and primes the roller to receive paint.

## LOADING A PAINT ROLLER

Pour ½ inch of paint into your plastic-lined paint pan. If necessary, attach your extension handle to your roller. (A 4-foot fiberglass extension handle works best.) Roll the dampened roller down the slope of the tray and into the well in quick motions to load the roller. The roller should be full but not dripping when you remove it from the tray.

## ROLLING ON PAINT

As with a brush, it is important to keep a wet edge when painting with a roller. Hold the roller so that the U-shaped end is away from the direction you are working. Work in small sections—about three or four roller widths—loading the roller with paint, then rolling up and down until the entire surface is covered. Work vertically from floor to ceiling, maintaining a firm, even pressure. Roll on paint with three strokes:

■ Unload the roller with an upward stroke.
■ Set the paint with a slightly lighter downward stroke.
■ Finish with a light upward stroke to smooth the paint and remove lines called snail trails.

Twisting the roller handle slightly in the direction you are working—normally to the right—helps eliminate lines. After you have painted about 8 feet of wall, lay off the paint to keep the sheen consistent. Do this by lightly rolling a damp roller from the top of the wall to the bottom.

### WALL WIZARD TIP

**WEATHER REPORT**
The weather can make a difference when you are painting. Paint goes on best when there's low humidity and average temperatures.

**PAINTING WITH A BRUSH**

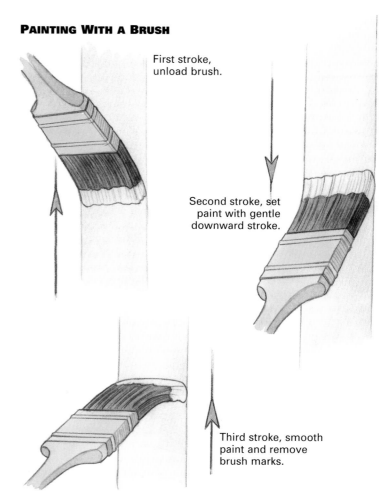

First stroke, unload brush.

Second stroke, set paint with gentle downward stroke.

Third stroke, smooth paint and remove brush marks.

**PAINTING WITH A ROLLER**

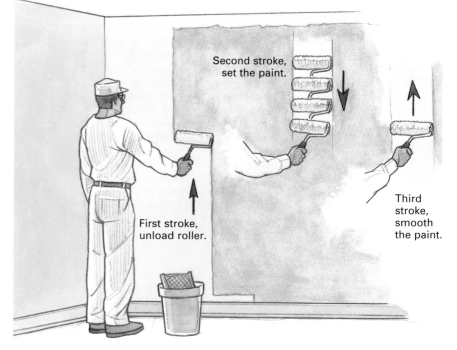

Second stroke, set the paint.

Third stroke, smooth the paint.

First stroke, unload roller.

# PAINTING WITH A SPRAYER

A paint sprayer can cover a large surface quickly. Today's high-volume, low-pressure (HVLP) paint sprayers drastically reduce overspray, which was one of the major drawbacks of spray painting inside a house. These sprayers are relatively easy to adjust and operate and apply a smooth, even coat. They produce a fine finish on small surfaces, such as furniture or cabinetry. Items that would be difficult or tedious to paint neatly with a brush or roller—louvered doors or heat grates, for instance—are easy to paint with a sprayer. A sprayer is also ideal for painting textured acoustical ceilings; some manufacturers offer a right-angle nozzle especially for ceilings.

Follow the sprayer manufacturer's instructions carefully. Here is the general procedure for spray painting:

**1.** Mask and drape surfaces and cover items in the room you don't want paint on. Even though HVLP sprayers minimize drift and overspray, there will be some.

**2.** Thin the paint to the consistency specified by the manufacturer. This ensures that the paint will atomize properly for a smooth finish. Manufacturers provide a viscosity cup or similar testing device to gauge the paint consistency—you fill the cup with paint and observe how long it takes to flow out through a hole in the bottom. Pour some paint into a bucket and thin it with the appropriate thinner to get the proper viscosity.

**3.** Strain the thinned paint as you pour it into the sprayer's paint cup. Straining helps prevent clogging and uneven painting.

**4.** Adjust the spray gun, following the manufacturer's instructions. Spray the paint onto a test piece of plywood or cardboard when making adjustments.

**5.** If the spray equipment is new to you, practice painting on a piece of plywood or cardboard first. To paint with the sprayer, hold the gun parallel to the floor with the nozzle perpendicular to the surface you're painting. The distance you hold the gun from the surface depends on the spray pattern and the size of the surface. In general, the farther away from the surface you hold the gun, the larger the area you will cover. The sprayer's instructions will give you advice. Keep the gun the same distance from the surface as you move it from side to side—don't swing the gun in an arc. Spray about a 20-inch-long pass. Pull the trigger after you start moving the gun and stop spraying before you stop moving the gun. This will prevent paint buildup and sags at the ends of the passes. Move the gun at a steady speed—the actual speed depends on the distance from the surface and the size of the spray pattern.

**6.** Build the color in several thin coats rather than applying one heavy coat. Overlap the passes to avoid streaks, runs, and sags.

**7.** Clean the spray equipment thoroughly immediately after use. Allowing paint to dry in the gun can clog it or cause it to spray unevenly.

**AEROSOL CANS:** If your job calls for a small amount of paint spraying—a room with one pair of louvered shutters, for instance—a can of aerosol paint might be all you need. Spray cans of paint can produce a fine surface if applied carefully. You probably won't be able to match a custom-mixed color, but you might find a color that's close enough.

Spray paint from an aerosol can the same way you would with a power sprayer: Keep the can parallel to the surface you're painting, apply thin coats, and overlap the passes. Depress the nozzle after you start moving the can and release it before you stop. A snap-on spray-can handle will give you better control and make the job easier.

Turn the can upside down and spray out paint to clear the nozzle after use. Dispose of empty aerosol cans properly.

**PAINTING WITH A SPRAYER**

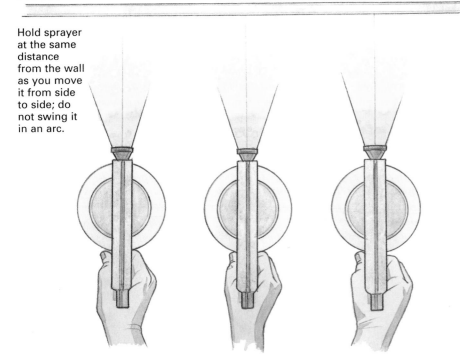

Hold sprayer at the same distance from the wall as you move it from side to side; do not swing it in an arc.

# PAINTING A ROOM

**CUTTING IN WITH A BRUSH**

Paint 3 to 4 inches out from corners and along edges and trim.

**CUTTING IN WITH A PAD**

Run edge of pad along trim.

Make the job go smoothly and ensure professional-looking results by following a specific sequence when you paint a room. First empty the room, then drape and mask it as described in the Final Steps in Preparation section beginning on page 55.

Start by painting the ceiling, then proceed to the walls and trim. Painting is best done with two people: One can do the cutting in with a brush or pad while the other paints the surfaces with a roller.

## CUTTING IN

Painters cut in—paint a narrow band with a brush or pad where one surface meets another—because a roller can't paint into a corner neatly or effectively. To cut in, paint a 3- to 4-inch-wide band along both sides of the inside corner between two walls, the ceiling and wall, or along a surface adjacent to trim or molding.

One of the worst mistakes in painting is cutting in an entire room, then rolling paint on the walls. This allows most of the cut-in bands to dry before you paint the wall, creating visible overlaps in the finish. To avoid a visible overlap, keep a wet edge where

you cut in so the paint flows together between the cut-in band and the roller-painted part of the wall. Cut in a short length of wall, roll the paint on, then cut in some more—about two roller widths.

**CUTTING IN WITH A PAD:** A paint pad is probably the easiest tool to use for cutting in a wall or ceiling. The pad will lay more paint on the surface than a brush. It also minimizes brush strokes and covers a surface much faster than brushing.

To load a paint pad, dip it in its tray, wiggle it around, and pat the pad to remove excess. To cut in, place the pad against the edge of the surface, and glide it along the corner.

### WALL WIZARD TIP

**COVER ROLLER ON BREAK**
When you take a break, lay your paint roller in the paint tray and cover the tray with plastic. Put paint pads in their storage containers with airtight lids and clean your brushes to keep them from drying out.

# PAINTING A ROOM
*continued*

## PAINTING THE CEILING

Begin by cutting in the ceiling. Using your trim brush, apply the paint in a 4-inch-wide band on the ceiling along the wall-ceiling line, and around any obstructions, such as light fixtures. Flex the bristles just enough to fan them out and create a straight edge. If you are working alone, cut in about 6 feet at a time to maintain a wet edge for painting sections with the roller, then alternate between cutting in and rolling.

Working from the corner farthest from the room's entry door, visually divide the ceiling into 6-foot-wide sections. Paint one section at a time, working in rows across the width of the room and toward the entry wall. Apply the paint by cutting in and rolling. Repeat these techniques, section by section, until the ceiling is completed.

Plan to finish the entire ceiling in one painting session. If you don't, the sections will dry at different times, leaving visible overlap marks. To avoid such flaws, always start a new section by overlapping the wet edge of the section just painted.

## PAINTING THE CEILING

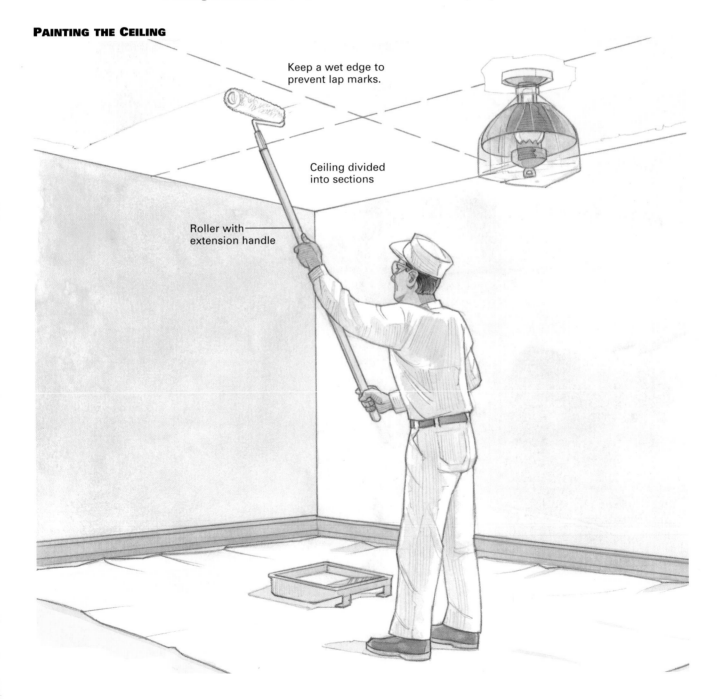

Keep a wet edge to prevent lap marks.

Ceiling divided into sections

Roller with extension handle

## PAINTING WALLS

Paint walls with a roller, working in sections three or four roller swaths wide. Paint walls with vertical strokes. Keep the edge wet and slightly overlap each section over the edge of the previous one as you paint. Move steadily and evenly with the paint while it is wet.

## PAINTING TRIM

Paint the trim—such as door and window casings, baseboards, and moldings—after the walls. Paint the trim with a painting pad or brush in the same way you would a surface. Paint moldings from the top of the room down. Work from left to right, always keeping a wet edge. Paint with the grain on woodwork. When painting the edge of a molding, protect the adjoining wall with a paint shield.

## PAINTING WINDOWS

Paint windows from the inside out. To keep paint off the glass, clean the pane, then apply lip balm around the edges. Heat it with a hair dryer and wipe it off after the paint dries. (Or, you can mask the glass with tape.) Paint from left to right or with the grain of the wood. The order in which you paint the parts of the window depends on the window style.

## WALL WIZARD TIP

### GO WITH THE GRAIN
Always paint with the grain. This means painting horizontal sections with horizontal strokes, and vertical sections with vertical strokes, working from the top down.

### PAINTING A DOUBLE-HUNG WINDOW

1. Paint across and then down the inside of the outside window.

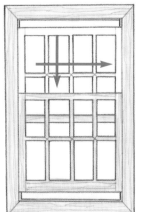

2. Paint across and then down the inside dividers of the outside window.

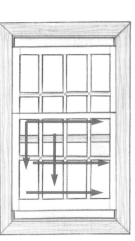

3. Paint across and then down on the outside frame and then across and down on the inside dividers of the inside window.

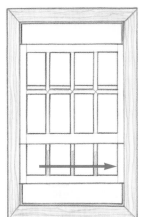

4. Push inside window up and pull outside window down; paint across bottom of outside window.

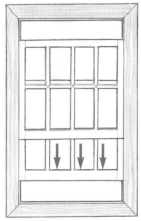

5. Paint down on the remaining parts of lower dividers on the outside.

6. Paint outer trim across and down sides.

## PAINTING A ROOM
*continued*

**PAINTING A FLUSH DOOR**

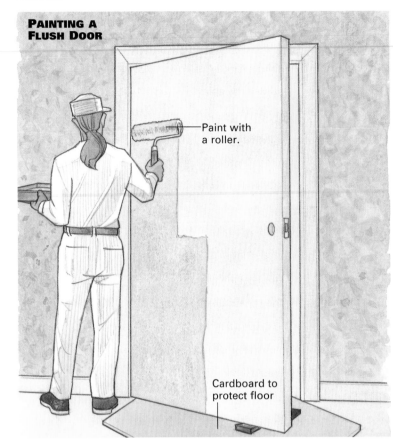

Paint with a roller.

Cardboard to protect floor

**PAINTING DOOR TRIM**

Casing

Stop

Jamb

Hinge masked with rubber cement

**PAINTING A PANELED DOOR**

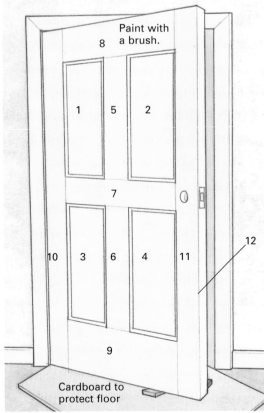

Paint with a brush.

Numbers show painting sequence.

Cardboard to protect floor

**PAINTING A PANEL**

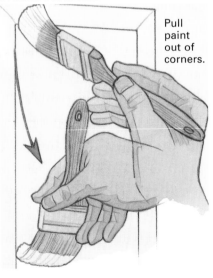

Pull paint out of corners.

### WALL WIZARD TIP

**CARDBOARD COVER-UP**
Slide a piece of cardboard underneath the door to protect the flooring.

## PAINTING DOORS

Doors are usually the last surface painted in a room. The easiest way to paint a door is to paint it in its frame. Remove the striker plate, door knobs, and other hardware, but leave the lock and hinges in place. Clean the lock and hinges with rubbing alcohol, then mask them with two thin coats of rubber cement.

**FLUSH DOORS:** Paint from left to right with a smooth-surface (¼-inch) roller, beginning on the inside of the room with the door closed. Paint two or three roller widths, then lay off the finish by brushing from bottom to top with an unloaded but damp brush. Paint around all sides of the door. When the paint is dry, score around the edges of the hinges and the lock with a knife and gently rub the rubber cement off.

**PANELED DOORS:** Paint paneled doors with a brush. Paint the panels first, starting with the panel moldings, moving to the recessed edge of the panel, and finishing with the face. Paint the center stiles (vertical members) and center rails (horizontal members) next. Next, paint the top and bottom rails, then the left and right stiles.

## ADJUSTABLE SHELVES, DRAWERS, AND CABINETS

Paint built-in bookcases and cabinetry after painting the walls. Start with adjustable shelves; remove them and lay them flat for easier painting. For a smooth finish, brush the paint. Place the shelves on supports while the paint dries so paint won't build up along edges or wick under the shelf onto the opposite surface. First paint the underside and back edge, then paint the top and leading edge. If the ends show, paint them along with one of the edges. Let each surface dry completely before painting the next.

Cabinet doors are easier to paint if you remove them. Remove all hinges and hardware. (You can leave doors attached and mask the hardware.) Paint the interior face of a door first, then coat the front and edges.

Remove drawers and stand them on their backs. Remove drawer pulls. Paint the drawer fronts and leading edges, but do not paint any other part of the drawer or the drawer openings inside the cabinet.

To paint a cabinet with nonremovable shelves, start at the back of the cabinet and move forward, following the sequence explained below and shown in the illustration. If the cabinet has drawers, remove them.

Paint the back wall first, followed by the shelf bottoms. Paint the side walls and shelf tops next, along with the leading edges of the shelves. Paint the floor of the cabinet next. Paint exposed end panels, then the horizontal members of the front face frame, followed by the vertical parts. Paint the inside of the door, then the outside and edges. Paint the toe kick last, if it is to be painted. Stand the drawers on their backs and paint the fronts only.

### WALL WIZARD TIP

#### NAILS MAKE BETTER SUPPORTS
When you remove doors and drawers from a cabinet, number them on the bottom for easy reinstallation. Then drive small brads into the bottom edge corners of each drawer front and door. Drive another brad into the upper inside left corner of each door. The brads support the parts while you paint them and while they dry.

### PAINTING A CABINET
Numbers show painting sequence.

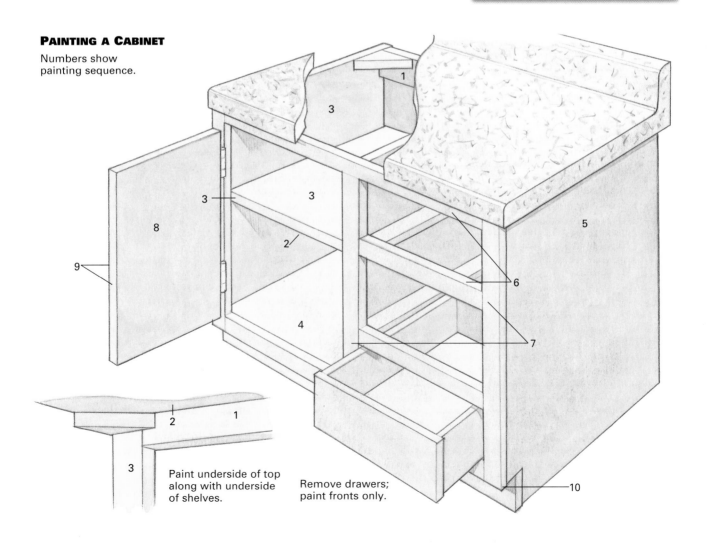

Paint underside of top along with underside of shelves.

Remove drawers; paint fronts only.

# PAINTING MASONRY

Painting masonry calls for special preparation and painting techniques because of alkali deposits, water seepage, and the coarsely textured, porous surface. Efflorescence—a white, powdery deposit frequently found on masonry surfaces—results when leaks allow moisture to migrate through concrete and mortar. It also can occur on new concrete due to normal hydration as the concrete cures. Wait at least six months for the concrete or mortar to cure before painting new concrete or masonry. Before painting old masonry, repair any active leaks and remove the deposits. (See page 48.) The surface must be clean and sound, so repair mortar joints and patch cracks and holes before painting.

Apply paint to masonry with a deep-nap roller cover or a large, thick-bristled brush. These tools will work the paint down into the rough texture. Most jobs require two coats—a sealer and finish color. To keep the sheen consistent and the surface smooth, back-brush by going over the surface in one direction.

Latex masonry paint works well on most masonry surfaces, including brick. However, there are many specialty masonry paints for surfaces such as floors and stairs. Check with your paint dealer.

*Proper preparation is the key to painting masonry. You can even paint old stone basement walls if you clean the surface carefully and ensure there are no leaks.*

## MORE PAINTING TIPS FROM THE WALL WIZARD

■ Paint pipes, wrought-iron balustrades, and other contoured surfaces with a paint glove, or mitt, or an HVLP spray gun.
■ A beveled paint roller helps prevent paint buildup in corners.
■ A bendable paint pad does a great job on fixed shutters, radiator fins, and other hard-to-reach surfaces.
■ Paint heating system registers and grills with aerosol paint.
■ When painting with enamel, work quickly and brush lightly. Overbrushing leaves streaks and marks; do not try to touch up areas you've already painted. If you have problems, let the

paint dry, degloss it, and repaint.
■ Wipe paint off your paint shield after each use to keep the edge clean.
■ Reduce paint odor by stirring in four drops of vanilla extract for each quart of latex paint. Peppermint oil also works, but do not use perfumes—they contain alcohol.
■ If bristles come off the brush, remove them from the painted surface with eyebrow tweezers or by touching them with the wet brush—they should cling to it. Wipe the brush with a clean cloth to remove stray bristles.
■ Work paint into deeply patterned woodwork with a foam brush.

# PAINTING FLOORS

Paint is an economical and attractive floor finish. A painted floor can be purely functional or an artistic expression. Wood or concrete floors are easily paintable. Resilient vinyl sheet and tile that are in good condition can be painted, although the embossed pattern will show through and the paint may not last very long. Glazed ceramic tile can't be painted.

## WHAT KIND OF PAINT?

You can paint floors with standard interior paint and enamel or more durable floor paint. Here's how they compare:
- Oil-base paint creates a hard film and covers a poorly prepared surface better.
- Latex paint gives a more resilient film. Because the paint film breathes, latex is more suitable in damp locations.
- Alkyd or modified epoxy latex porch and floor paint dries to a durable surface, but color selection is limited.
- Industrial enamel is tough. The high gloss make the surface slippery, but you can add nonslip grit to the paint.
- Porcelain-epoxy paint is the most durable. Some lighter colors have a satin finish.

## WOOD FLOORS

Prepare a wood floor as you would other woodwork—scrape off loose paint, then repair and smooth the surface. Vacuum the floor. If the floor is bare wood or has bare spots, apply a sealer (see page 58), otherwise use primer. Roll or brush on the finish coat, working from the farthest corner to the doorway.

## CONCRETE FLOORS

Concrete takes a little more preparation. Here are the steps:
- Make sure the slab is clean and dry. Let new concrete cure for at least six months before painting.
- Patch cracks and uneven joints with an expansive mortar. Allow it to cure, following the manufacturer's instructions.
- Scrape off loose or flaking paint. If the old paint job is rough all over, scrape or strip it off.
- Scrub the floor with trisodium phosphate (TSP) mixed with water, according to instructions.
- Etch the concrete with a solution of one part muriatic acid added to 10 parts water if you are using oil-base paint. Use phosphoric acid solution in the same ratio for latex paint. Both acids are dangerous; mix the solution in a plastic pail, adding the acid to the water—

*These carpets aren't real; they're painted on a wood floor.*

never pour water into acid; it can boil and splash out. Wear rubber gloves and safety goggles while mixing and applying, and follow all instructions on the container.
- Let the floor dry, then vacuum up the dust.
- Apply sealer (not necessary if you paint with acrylic latex paint or alkyd porch and floor enamel). Roll or brush the finish coat.

## VINYL FLOORING

Before painting the whole floor, paint a hidden spot to make sure you'll like the look. Paint only sound vinyl; flooring that's dented or has holes in it should be removed. Prepare the vinyl by sanding with medium-grit sandpaper to dull the shine. Clean up all the sanding dust, then apply a liquid deglosser to improve bonding. Apply primer. Roll or brush on one or two finish coats.

*The embossed pattern shows when you paint vinyl flooring (below). The pattern does not distract from the checkerboard design painted on this flooring, but it might clash with a free-form design.*

# TEXTURE COMPOUND

*A roller with 1¼-inch-deep nap stipples the surface. Vary direction and pressure for a random pattern.*

*Dab, drag, or swirl a sponge on the surface to create a pattern. A sponge with large holes works best.*

*Swirl circular loops into the surface with a whisk broom or wallpaper brush. Overlap the swirls.*

*Dab the surface with a dry paintbrush in short, quick patting motions to create a ridged texture.*

*Crumple paper or a rag and pat it over the surface. Pressure and direction will vary the pattern.*

*When the paint is nearly dry, you can knock the points off any pattern with a trowel or broad knife.*

Thick-bodied texture compound—sometimes called texture paint—lets you give smooth surfaces the look of stucco or masonry. The material also effectively covers problem walls or ceilings, those with uneven surfaces, rough spots, and other flaws. Texture compounds are available premixed in smooth- and rough-texture finishes and coarse ceiling textures.

The texture to use depends on the size of the room and the desired effect; ask your paint dealer. Texture additives, including an antiskid material for floors and stairs, can be mixed into standard latex paints.

Apply texture compound with a trowel or 10-inch broad knife. Put it on about ¼ inch thick. After applying the texture material, you can work it with a brush, sponge, rag, or roller to create special effects. Going over a just-textured surface with a trowel or broad knife will knock the peaks off the texture for a different look. Make trial applications on foot-square pieces of plywood, particleboard, or drywall to work out the application and tooling that give a texture you like. To paint the textured wall, apply two coats of oil-base sealer. Let that dry, then apply the finish coat.

# STORING AND DISPOSING OF PAINT

You will probably have paint left over after you complete the job. Store paint properly for future touch-ups and repairs. You'll need to throw out some materials too. This can require a trip to your local hazardous-waste disposal facility. Rags you have used with oil-base paints can catch fire through spontaneous combustion while they are damp; spread them out to dry—don't wad them up—before disposal.

## STORING PAINT

Store leftover paint in tightly sealed cans. Here's how to seal it to prevent drying and skinning over.

**1.** Clean paint from the rim well and sides of the can. Cut a disc from a plastic garbage bag about 1 inch larger in diameter than the paint can. The plastic serves as a gasket to prevent metal-to-metal corrosion. It also plugs the holes punched into the can rim (see page 59), and allows you to scrape settled pigments back into the paint upon reopening.

**2.** Spray nonstick kitchen vegetable spray on the paint side of the plastic to keep the lid well wet and to seal the lid. It also helps keep skin from forming on the paint.

**3.** Exhale into the can three times; the carbon dioxide from your breath will displace the oxygen in the can.

**4.** Place the plastic gasket over the opening, sprayed side down, and gently tap the lid closed. Do not distort the lid by hammering.

**5.** Store the paint can upside down. This keeps air from seeping into the can. Store the paint where it won't freeze.

## DISPOSAL

Most paint products are considered hazardous and require proper disposal—taking them to an authorized household hazardous waste disposal site. Don't pour them down the drain, into a storm sewer, onto the ground, or into the trash. Call your local solid waste disposal office for exact information. To get rid of old water-base paint, spread the paint on a large sheet of plastic, let it dry, then throw the entire sheet into the trash. Leave the lids off empty latex paint cans until the paint residue dries. You can then safely throw the cans in the trash.

Pour water-base cleaning solutions into a compost pile where they can be broken down in the soil. You can also pour the solution throughout your garden or dispose of it at your local solid waste disposal center. Petroleum-base solvents must be taken to a hazardous waste disposal facility. Let used thinners sit undisturbed for a time; the paint pigment will settle to the bottom, then you can pour off the clear thinner and reuse it.

Hang oil- or solvent-soaked rags outdoors to dry. Wadding them up makes spontaneous combustion more likely. Never store solvent-soaked materials indoors. They catch fire easily and can release harmful fumes.

WALL WIZARD TIP

For quick touch-ups, pour a small amount of paint into a small glass jar, close it tightly, and label it to identify the room it's for. You can also store extra paint in clean shoe polish applicators—the pads are perfect for small jobs.

*Store partial cans of paint upside down to prevent skinning over and drying. A gasket cut from a plastic garbage bag fits between the lid and the can.*

*Let empty latex paint cans dry, then throw them away with the trash.*

# WALLPAPERING BASICS

You'll probably be able to wallpaper a standard-size room in one day or less by following the techniques described in this chapter.

If you have never installed wallpaper, start with a simple room—one with flat walls and few doors and windows—or a room where errors won't be apparent. A child's room or laundry room is a better place for your first wallpapering project than the more visible living room or kitchen. With a little practice, you can tackle more prominent rooms with confidence.

Two installers are better than one. A coordinated effort—one person cutting and prepping the paper, and the other person putting it on the wall—makes wallpapering easy.

**Various wallpaper patterns in coordinated colors contribute to the charm of this suite. A chair rail separates the floral pattern and stripes in the bedroom; another lively pattern brightens the sitting area.**

# LAYING OUT THE JOB

**WALLPAPER LAYOUT**

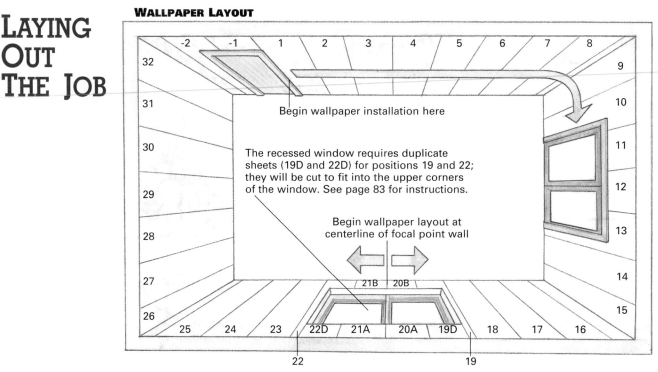

Begin wallpaper installation here

The recessed window requires duplicate sheets (19D and 22D) for positions 19 and 22; they will be cut to fit into the upper corners of the window. See page 83 for instructions.

Begin wallpaper layout at centerline of focal point wall

A professional-looking wallcovering job calls for a well-planned layout that shows where each sheet will go on the walls. Without such planning, you may end up with awkward seam locations, strips of wallcovering too narrow for proper adhesion, pattern mismatches in conspicuous places, or a strong wallcovering pattern that feels out of balance with the room's focal point. To avoid such problems, follow these three planning principles:

■ Start the layout at the vertical centerline of the room's focal-point wall. From this starting point, the pattern will flow evenly across this wall and on around the room.
■ Put the last seam, which usually mismatches, in the dead corner—the most inconspicuous spot in the room. Common dead corners include corners behind doors, the header space above the entrance door, and hidden alcoves.
■ Reduce the number of full-length seams in the room by planning the layout to place seams near the center of windows and doors. Try to leave at least half a sheet—or at least a strip wider than 6 inches—on each side of a door or window.

## FINDING THE FOCAL POINT

The first layout you develop may not satisfy all of these principles. There are other factors, such as corners, to consider. You may need to make adjustments through a process of trial and error. The starting point for the layout, however, should always be the centerline of the focal-point wall.

To begin the layout, stand in the doorway and look for the room's focal point. The focal point is probably one of the following:
■ The first wall you see as you enter the room. The centerline runs down its middle.
■ The room's main window or windows (often located opposite the door). If there is only one window, no matter what its size, it becomes the focal point and the centerline runs down its center. If there is more than one window but they are on different walls, the larger window is the focal point. If there are two or more windows set close together or side by side, the focal-point centerline lies midway between them. If you have corner windows, or windows near the corner on two adjoining walls, they make a focal corner. The centerline runs through the center of the window closest to that corner, or through the largest window.
■ The portion of wall above a fireplace.
■ The largest section of exposed wall in a bathroom or kitchen.
■ The main section of wall in a kitchen eating area.

Your layout starts at the vertical centerline of this wall. Once you identify the focal point of the room, use a No.1 pencil to lightly mark the centerline at eye level. This becomes the starting point for planning a trial layout of sheet positions, but it is not the point where you will start hanging wallpaper.

## WHERE TO BEGIN INSTALLATION

The wallpaper should match perfectly at the focal point of the room. So hanging the first sheet at the focal point could pose a problem: Chances are that the wallpaper edge would dry by the time you worked your way around the room so it would be difficult to adjust, and the pattern wouldn't match. To prevent that, move the starting point from the focal point back to the dead corner, usually near the door—behind an open door is ideal. You probably won't see the mismatch if the pattern doesn't align in this corner.

## POSITIONING WALLPAPER SHEETS

Once you've determined your focal point and your physical starting point for hanging wallpaper in a room, it's time to determine where each sheet of wallpaper will be hung. Here's how to do it:

**1.** Center the first sheet over the centerline of your focal point or align one edge with the centerline, whichever works best. Then, measure and mark the seams lightly with a lead pencil for the rest of the room, adding ⅛ inch on average to allow for expansion when the paper is wet. Work from the corners of the focal-point wall to the dead corner.

**2.** Working from left to right, begin numbering the spaces between the marked seams in the order in which they will be hung. For example, the first full-height strip will be sheet 1. This master sheet is the first you will hang, and it is the master pattern to which all other sheets will be matched.

**3.** Working from left to right, continue numbering the sheet positions around the room to the dead corner (+2, +3, and so on). When you come to wide windows or other openings where you will split a sheet in two, label the upper section A and the bottom section B. Number the sheets between the dead corner and the edge of the first sheet of wallpaper with negative numbers because those sheets will be hung from right to left instead of following the left-to-right rule.

**4.** Once you have numbered each sheet location on the wall, measure the actual height of the wall in each slot in sequence, and add 4 inches. This is selvage; it allows for waste and

### ADJUSTING LAYOUT FOR WINDOWS

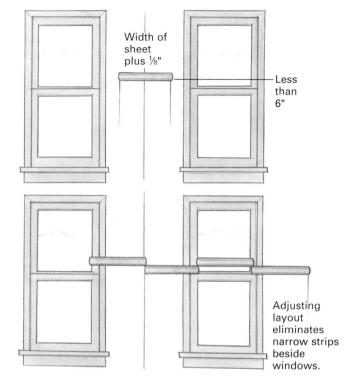

Width of sheet plus ⅛"

Less than 6"

Adjusting layout eliminates narrow strips beside windows.

trimming. List each sheet number and its length on a piece of paper; this worksheet will guide you throughout installation.

**5.** Recessed windows or similar openings require duplicate sheets, marked D on the layout. (See page 83.)

### ADJUSTING LAYOUT FOR CORNERS

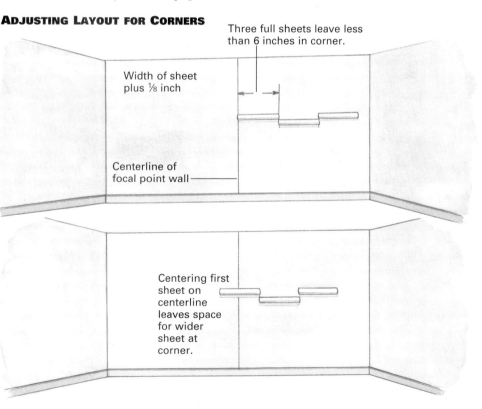

Three full sheets leave less than 6 inches in corner.

Width of sheet plus ⅛ inch

Centerline of focal point wall

Centering first sheet on centerline leaves space for wider sheet at corner.

# PREPARING THE WALLPAPER

## CUTTING WALLPAPER

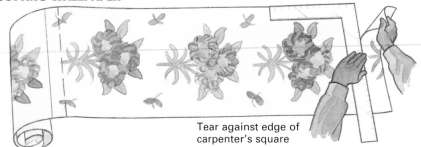

Tear against edge of carpenter's square

## REVERSE HANGING

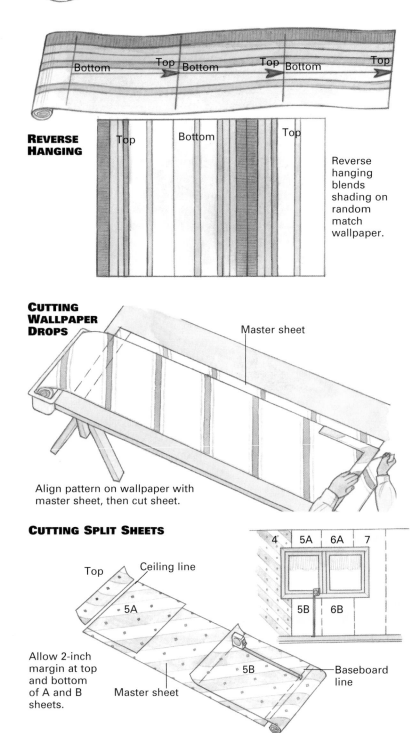

Bottom   Top   Bottom   Top   Bottom   Top

Top   Bottom   Top

Reverse hanging blends shading on random match wallpaper.

## CUTTING WALLPAPER DROPS

Master sheet

Align pattern on wallpaper with master sheet, then cut sheet.

## CUTTING SPLIT SHEETS

Top   Ceiling line

5A

Allow 2-inch margin at top and bottom of A and B sheets.

Master sheet

5B

4   5A   6A   7

5B   6B

Baseboard line

How wallpaper is cut depends on its pattern. And though the operation is called cutting, the material is actually torn against a straightedge. Save waste pieces in a plastic bag for finishing touches and repairs.

To cut wallpaper, align the short edge of a carpenter's square with the edge of the wallcovering. Press down firmly on the carpenter's square, and tear away the paper toward the wide blade of the square as shown in the illustration at left. Add a 2-inch margin at the top and bottom of each sheet to allow for irregularities in the ceiling and floor.

**RANDOM MATCH:** Because there is no repeating horizontal pattern, you can cut sheets of wallpaper continuously off the roll. Random-match wallpaper is reverse-hung: The bottom of every other sheet is placed near the ceiling.

**STRAIGHT ACROSS MATCH:** Cut the master sheet of wallpaper to the length shown on your worksheet for position No. 1. For each additional sheet, align the pattern along the seam edge of the master sheet. Slide the paper on top of the master sheet to about 1 inch from the left edge, and cut. Number each sheet lightly on the top left corner.

To tear the upper section (A) for a split sheet, align the top edge of the wallpaper roll with the top edge of the previous sheet, then tear to the measurement shown on your layout guide. The A sheets are measured from the top of the master sheet down.

To tear the B sheets, align the edge of the wallpaper roll with the bottom edge of the previous sheet, then tear to the measurement from your layout guide. The B sheets are measured against the master sheet from the bottom up.

**DROP MATCH:** Drop-match patterns are cut in a different way than straight-across match patterns: There are two master sheets—odd and even. Tear your first master sheet to the proper length for position No. 1. This sheet is the odd master sheet. Cut the next sheet, for position No. 2, to correctly match the pattern. The second sheet is the even master sheet. When labeling the sheets and marking them on your worksheet, mark them 1-O for odd, 2-E for even, and so on. Each subsequent sheet that you cut should match either the odd or even master sheet. Cut each sheet to length for the space it will fit.

# PROCESSING THE WALLPAPER

After the wallpaper is cut, labeled, and laid on the worktable, it's ready for processing. Process the paper in two steps.

■ **BACKROLLING:** Roll each individual sheet so that the pattern is on the inside. Make sure the number on the outside of the sheet is visible, then secure the roll with a large rubber band. Backrolling takes the twist out of the paper and exposes the pasted side, making it easier to activate. The number on the back of the sheet is easy to see too, and the cylinder is easier to handle than a sheet.

■ **SEQUENCING:** The next step is lining up the paper in the order it will be hung. If you can't hang the paper the day you cut and backroll it, store the rolls in a plastic bag, then sequence the wallpaper when you're ready to hang it.

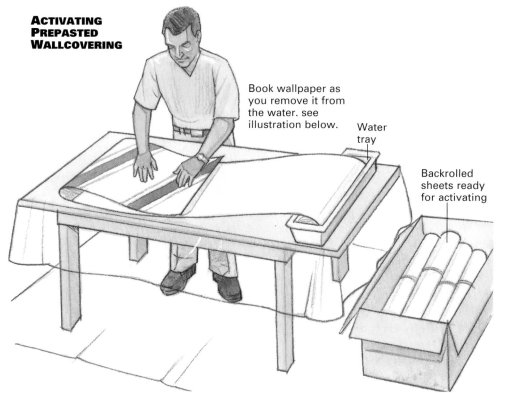

**ACTIVATING PREPASTED WALLCOVERING**

Book wallpaper as you remove it from the water. see illustration below.

Water tray

Backrolled sheets ready for activating

## BOOKING

Before installing the wallpaper, you must activate prepasted wallpaper or apply adhesive to nonpasted paper. An important part of this operation is booking (folding) the wallpaper, as shown at right. Booking keeps the paste from drying out and prevents debris from contaminating the adhesive. It allows moisture to soak fully and evenly into the backing to promote better adhesion. Proper booking allows the wallcovering to expand evenly. It also makes the wallpaper easier to handle during installation. To speed up the job, one person can activate (or apply paste)

**BOOKING WALLCOVERING**

Overlap ends 1 inch.

Pasted side to inside

Fold wallpaper but do not crease it.

Fold wallpaper but do not crease it.

## WALL WIZARD TIP

### INSPECT THE WALLCOVERING
Before installing wallcoverings, inspect the material. Check each bolt's pattern and dye lot number to make sure they match; if they don't, exchange them for rolls that do. Open and reroll each bolt to check for printing flaws; look for consistency in pattern, color, and surface finish. Also watch for ink blobs or smudges, streaks, wrinkling, pattern shifts, or obvious misalignments.

# PROCESSING THE WALLPAPER
*continued*

and book the wallcovering while another installs it. Here are the steps for activating or applying adhesive:

## PREPASTED WALLCOVERING

**1.** Fill a plastic garden planter box (water tray) three-fourths full of water at 72 to 80 degrees. Warmer water will cook the adhesive and overexpand the paper; cooler water won't penetrate and activate the adhesive.

**2.** Remove the rubber band and loosen the first sheet so water can get between the layers. Soak the sheet in the water according to the manufacturer's instructions, timing it carefully. Oversoaking dissolves adhesive; undersoaking doesn't activate the adhesive.

**3.** Grab each corner of the strip and slowly pull three-fourths of its length from the water tray, paste side up. Check the back for uniform wetness, and splash any dry spots with water from the tray.

**4.** Fold the top edge of the strip to the middle of the sheet, the pasted faces together. Align the edges, or seams, and smooth, but do not crease the fold.

**5.** Slowly pull out the rest of the sheet. Check it for wetness and wet dry spots as necessary. Fold the bottom up and tuck it under the top edge so the ends overlap about 1 inch. This keeps the ends and middle of the sheet from drying out. Align and smooth as you did the top section.

**6.** To book the wallpaper, fold the farthest fold to the fold nearest the water tray. Repeat. The sheet is now booked. Stack the booked

sheets on a towel on the floor beside the work table. Activate and book five more strips to make a stack of six. Repeat for all sheets, working in sequence. Let activated sheets sit 5 to 15 minutes.

**7.** Flip the stack over. This puts the first sheet back on top. Wrap the stack in a towel and carry it to the room you're wallpapering.

## NONPASTED WALLCOVERING

Nonpasted wallcovering is not immersed in water, so there isn't as much moisture in the paper as in prepasted wallcovering. Because of this, adhesive is applied in two steps to allow the paper to absorb the moisture necessary for good adhesion. Use a clear, nonstaining premixed vinyl wallcovering adhesive. Thin the adhesive to spreading consistency in accordance with the manufacturer's instructions. The usual recommendation is to mix 2 to 3 cups of water into 2 gallons of premixed paste until it has the consistency of pancake batter. Mix the adhesive in a 5-gallon bucket with a whisk or a propeller mixer in a power drill.

**1.** Apply the adhesive with a foam or sponge roller. Load the roller with paste as you would with paint.

**2.** Unroll the first sheet face down on the table. Roll paste onto the edges along the full length of the sheet.

**3.** Roll paste across the width of the covering, working from the center out to the edge of the area to be pasted. Apply it in overlapping zigzag strokes until you thoroughly coat the sheet. Finish by rolling one more coat along the edges.

**4.** Book the sheet the same way as prepasted covering.

**5.** Paste and book just one or two more sheets. Nonpasted coverings absorb moisture from the adhesive, causing it to dry more quickly.

**6.** Flip the sheets over so the first is on top. Slip them into a plastic bag to hold in the moisture longer.

**APPLYING ADHESIVE TO NONPASTED WALLCOVERING**

Roll adhesive onto edges first

Apply second coat to edges

Coat sheet with adhesive, rolling from side to side

# INSTALLING WALLPAPER

A sheet of wallcovering changes its name and becomes a drop when you hang it on a wall. Wallpaper is easier to install and adheres better if you handle it gently. Don't push, pull, shove, or press it into place to get a good seal; rough handling stretches the material and pushes the adhesive out of place, causing wavy seams that are more visible and corners that are more likely to pull away from the wall after they dry. Wallpaper dries in three to five days.

## THREE RULES FOR WALLPAPERING

Here are three basic rules to remember as you install wallcoverings:

■ Every time you start on a new wall, snap a new plumb line. This keeps the paper straight. Use yellow chalk—blue chalk bleeds through the seams—and lightly brush away excess chalk. Snap the line on the wall, where the right side of the first sheet will be.

■ Cut inside corners and wrap outside corners. Walls often are not square to each other, so folding a sheet around an inside corner can cause puckering and introduce crookedness. Outside corners are wrapped to avoid having an exposed cut edge that can lift or tear at the corner. Don't worry about

pattern mismatches in corners; a corner is rarely looked at closely, so it's a perfect place to make up for out-of-square walls.

■ Do not overlap wallpaper. Seams must butt together tightly to be invisible and for the pattern to match. Also, wallpaper doesn't stick to itself well—overlapped seams will come loose.

## THE BASIC INSTALLATION TECHNIQUE

Every sheet of wallpaper goes on the wall in the same way. Place the ladder directly in front of the space where the first sheet will go. Put the 6-inch broad knife, smoothing brush, and snap-off tip knives in your apron pockets. Hang the first sheet, then additional sheets in sequence. Here are the steps to follow:

**1.** Climb the ladder and unfold the top portion of the booked drop. The folded bottom acts as a weight to hold the sheet straight. Align the edge of the sheet so that a 2-inch margin overlaps the ceiling. Position the key element as desired.

### WALL WIZARD TIP

#### FIX WRINKLES, NOT BUBBLES
No matter how tempted you may be to pop a bubble in a drop, leave it alone. Adhesive generates bubbles through chemical action with water. As soon as the water content decreases through drying, the bubbles will go away. If there are wrinkles, immediately lift the drop and adjust it until it hangs straight.

**INSTALLING WALLCOVERING**

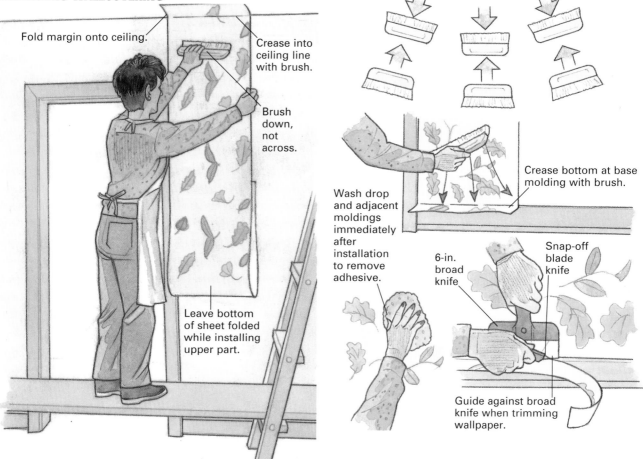

Fold margin onto ceiling.

Crease into ceiling line with brush.

Brush down, not across.

Leave bottom of sheet folded while installing upper part.

Wash drop and adjacent moldings immediately after installation to remove adhesive.

Crease bottom at base molding with brush.

6-in. broad knife

Snap-off blade knife

Guide against broad knife when trimming wallpaper.

# INSTALLING WALLPAPER

*continued*

## SETTING A SEAM

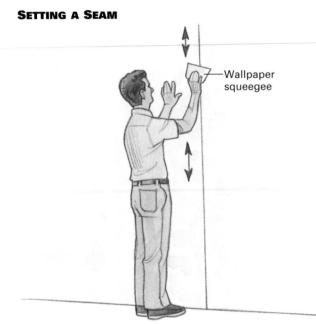

Wallpaper squeegee

## DOUBLE-CUT SEAM

Overlap wallpaper, match pattern

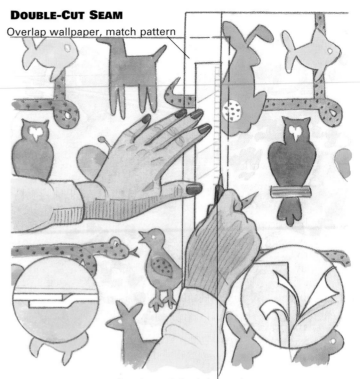

Cut through both layers in one pass.

**2.** Tap the sheet into the ceiling line with the wallpapering brush so the 2-inch margin flaps over onto the ceiling. Then smooth the paper on the wall with downward strokes of the brush.

**3.** Climb down and move the ladder out of the way. Open the bottom half of the sheet and smooth the bottom of the drop against the wall with the brush. Crease the wallpaper into the base molding so the 2-inch margin overlaps the baseboard.

**4.** Using the broad knife as a guide, trim off the excess paper at the ceiling and baseboard with a cutting knife. Start with a new snap-off knife tip for each cut. As you trim, slide the broad knife along the cut without lifting the cutting knife tip from the wallpaper.

**5.** Gently lift the edge and wipe away the chalk line. Smooth the edge back into place with the brush. Then brush the entire sheet one more time. If some bubbles won't work out, don't worry about them now. Most will disappear as the covering shrinks when drying. Remember that the goal is to eliminate air—not adhesive. Continue hanging drops around the room.

**6.** After installing two or three drops, wash the wall and molding with clear water and a sponge to remove adhesive residue. Wash from the top down. Dry the wall with a towel to reduce water-spotting.

## WALL WIZARD TIP

### DIFFERENT ADHESIVES

Don't try to install prepasted wallpaper using adhesive for nonpasted paper. The two adhesives aren't compatible and the wallpaper won't stick well to the wall.

## SEAMS

Tight-fitting seams are the key to successful wallpapering; they are nearly invisible, giving continuity of pattern and rhythm. Don't overlap sheets—the seam won't adhere well and the pattern will not align. There are the two types of seams:

■ The butt seam is the most common wallpaper seam. The sheets butt snugly against one another edge to edge. Don't stretch the material or the sheets will pull away from each other as the covering dries.

■ The double-cut seam is used for special situations, such as outside corners and borders. This seam starts with overlapping sheets. Using a carpenter's square or a straightedge as a guide, cut through both layers with the knife. Make the cut from the ceiling to the baseboard without cutting into the wall. Throw away the scrap from the sheet on top. Carefully lift the edge of that sheet and pull out the scrap from the sheet underneath. The two sheets will now butt together along the cut edges, and the pattern will match. Gently smooth the seam with your brush.

**SETTING SEAMS:** To set a seam, brush it with a wallpaper-smoothing brush to eliminate air. Gently tap the seam with the bristle edge of the brush to tighten the bond. Then, lightly pull a plastic squeegee up and down across the seam instead of rolling it— a seam roller squeezes out the adhesive. The squeegee levels the seam without squeezing

## WALLPAPERING AN INSIDE CORNER

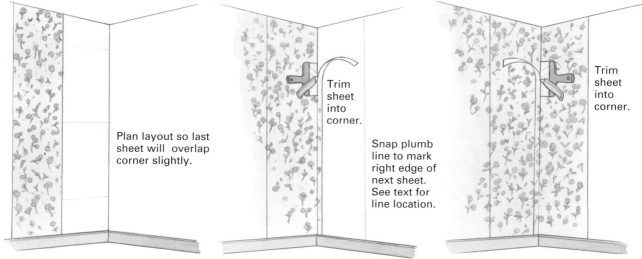

Plan layout so last sheet will overlap corner slightly.

Trim sheet into corner.

Snap plumb line to mark right edge of next sheet. See text for line location.

Trim sheet into corner.

out the adhesive. Always work vertically; going horizontally across the seam will pull the wallpaper out of alignment.

### GOING AROUND CORNERS

Trim the wallpaper into inside corners, such as at the ceiling joint, wall corners, when meeting moldings, and in similar places. Some of the pattern is lost in trimming, so the pattern rarely matches in inside corners.

Wrapping outside corners prevents the paper from lifting off the wall at the corner and keeps the pattern continuous. Examples of wrapped corners include an outside wall corner, perhaps from an entry to the hall, or a recessed window opening without moldings.

### CUTTING INSIDE CORNERS

When hanging the last sheet on a wall into a corner, the paper should be split into two separate pieces. This prevents the paper from buckling and wrinkling in the corner, and keeps the pattern aligned vertically, though not always perfectly matched. Here's how to make the corner:

**1.** Install the left side of the wallpaper sheet on the wall coming into the corner. Let the right side overlap onto the other wall.

**2.** Crease the wallpaper into the corner. Using a 6-inch plastic wallpaper squeegee as a guide, trim the sheet to the corner. Then remove the piece that laps onto the next wall.

**3.** Measure the width of the leftover piece. Subtract 1/4 inch,

then snap a plumb line on the new wall at this distance from the corner.

**4.** Place the leftover piece alongside the new plumb line so the pattern is vertical and aligned as well as possible. Trim the overlap from the left wall.

### COVERING OUTSIDE CORNERS

**1.** Hang the drop that goes around the corner, smoothing it up to and around the edge of the corner. Make tension cuts in the 2-inch margin at the top and bottom where they bend around the corner.

**2.** Measure the width at the top, middle, and bottom of the part of the sheet that has been wrapped around the corner. Subtract 3/8 inch from the narrowest width measurement and lightly mark the wallpaper that distance from the corner.

## WALLPAPERING AN OUTSIDE CORNER

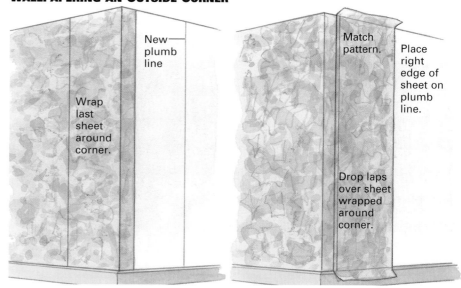

New plumb line

Wrap last sheet around corner.

Match pattern.

Place right edge of sheet on plumb line.

Drop laps over sheet wrapped around corner.

# INSTALLING WALLPAPER
*continued*

**3.** Measure the width of the next drop from the mark on the wallpaper, and strike a plumb line on the wall at that point.

**4.** Set the sheet directly on this plumb line so the pattern is realigned. Smooth into place, letting the drop lap over the sheet wrapped around the corner.

**5.** Using a carpenter's square or a straightedge as a guide, make a double-cut seam to remove the overlap. Set the seam.

## ENDING AT AN OUTSIDE CORNER

If you want to end the wallpaper at an outside corner, start by installing the wallpaper as if you were going to go around the corner, but let the excess extend past the corner instead of smoothing it down. Hold the excess wallcovering taut with one hand and, holding your knife at a 45-degree angle and cutting from the face side, make a sliding cut down the corner. This leaves a clean edge that won't fray or peel.

## WALLPAPERING AROUND TRIMMED DOORS AND WINDOWS

Instead of trying to precut a sheet to fit around a door, window, or other opening, hang a full-length drop over the opening and trim it. Here's how to do that:

**1.** Hang the drop, leaving the bottom half booked. With your smoothing brush press the covering against the top and sides of the trim molding around the opening. The paper should now hang over the opening.

**2.** If there is a large amount of wallcovering over the opening, cut away most of the excess at the top half of the opening to get it out of

**WALLPAPERING AROUND
A TRIMMED OPENING**

Install full sheet; let excess hang over opening.

Make sliding cut along molding with broad knife and wallpaper knife.

Make tension cuts at corners with scissors.

Trim wallpaper around sill, apron, or other molding as needed.

your way. Then, cut from the top corner of the molding with scissors to the edge of the wallpaper at a 45-degree angle. This is called a tension cut.

**3.** Drop the bottom half of the covering and repeat steps 1 and 2. For a window, trim away the remaining excess over the window and make a tension cut into the bottom corner at a 45-degree angle. Cut away the excess over a door opening down to the floor.

**4.** Use a broad knife to score the wallpaper along the trim molding around the opening. Trim off the excess wallpaper.

## WALLPAPERING AROUND RECESSED WINDOWS AND DOORS

Windows, doorways, wall niches, and other openings without moldings around them call for a different treatment. Here's how to wallpaper a window; follow the same procedures for other openings. You will need a duplicate sheet for the sheet at each side of the window. The pattern on the duplicate matches the sheet at the side of the opening (19 in illustration), but is only as long as the top part of the split sheet (20A).

**1.** Hang the wallpaper around the window (sheets 19 and 20A). Do not trim the excess from the side sheet (19); wrap the top sheet (20A) into the opening.

**2.** At the side, hold the excess material taut with one hand while you make a sliding cut along the top edge of the opening to the corner. Then wrap the excess paper on the side into the opening.

**3.** Smooth the wallpaper inside the opening and trim off the excess.

**4.** Working down around the window, make a series of small tension cuts into the paper around the window sill. Trim off the excess. Smooth and trim.

**5.** Once the paper is hung, the wall will be exposed on the underside of the recess at the top corners of the window. Measure in 1 inch from one corner and, using a carpenter's square as a guide, cut through the wallcovering from the ceiling down to the opening edge. Remove the strip of wallpaper above the window. Repeat on the other side.

**6.** Measure the distance from the inside seam at the top of the window to the corner; add 1 inch. Using this measurement, split the precut duplicate sheet to this width, realigning the pattern. Measure from the right edge of the sheet on the left side of the window (19D), the left edge of the sheet on the right side of the window. Hang the paper, then make a tension cut out and away from the corner; trim. This allows the wallpaper to fit inside the recess.

**7.** Using the carpenter's square as a guide,

make a double-cut seam from the ceiling down to the window corner. Trim and remove the excess.

**8.** Repeat on the other side of the opening.

### WALLPAPERING A RECESSED OPENING

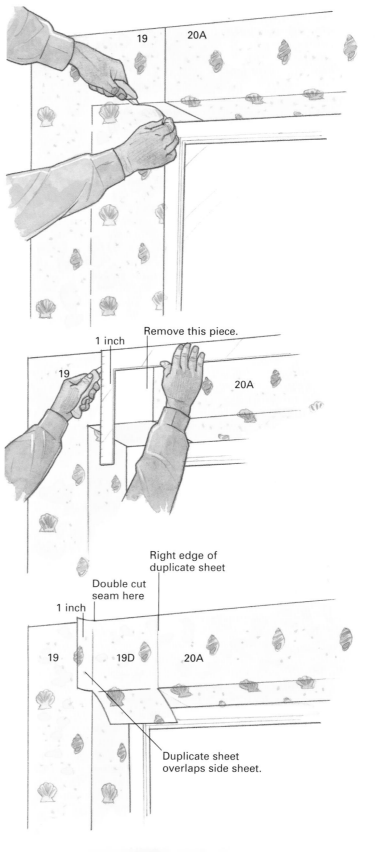

1 inch

Remove this piece.

19

20A

Right edge of duplicate sheet

Double cut seam here

1 inch

19    19D    20A

Duplicate sheet overlaps side sheet.

# TRIMMING TECHNIQUES

### TRIMMING AROUND A RECTANGULAR BOX

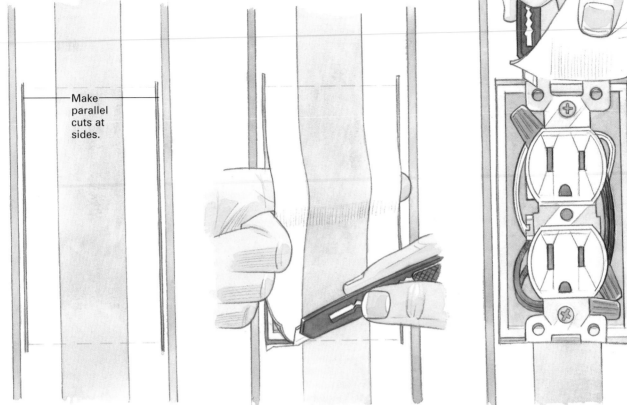

Make parallel cuts at sides.

### TRIMMING AROUND LIGHT FIXTURE BOX

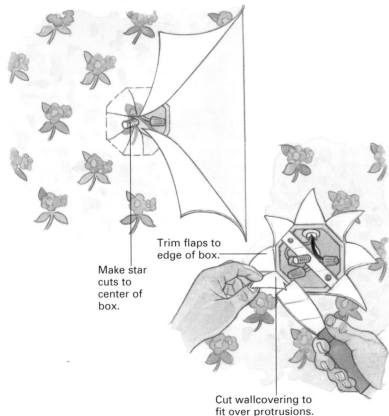

Make star cuts to center of box.

Trim flaps to edge of box.

Cut wallcovering to fit over protrusions.

You will find electrical switches and outlets in any room you wallpaper. There may also be light fixtures, plumbing fixtures, or heating and ventilating grilles in the walls you are covering. Here are some tips on dealing with them.

## ELECTRICAL SWITCHES AND OUTLETS

Turn off electricity to the room you're wallpapering at the circuit breaker box before starting the installation. Remove switch and outlet cover plates as part of the preparation for the project. Make sure water doesn't get into electrical boxes as you work. Water in a switch or outlet could pose hazards when you restore power.

As with door and window openings, install wallpaper right over the switch or outlet and smooth it in place all around. In the opening, make a vertical cut with the wallpaper knife parallel to the right side of the outlet and another on the left side. Pull the tab outward, then cut across the bottom to join the two slits. Cut away the tab at the top, and trim the wallpaper to the edge of the opening on all sides. Lift and smooth the paper around the switch or outlet.

## REMOVABLE LIGHT FIXTURES

If you removed the entire fixture and mounting canopy when you prepped the room, only the electrical box remains in place. (The electricity should be off.) Install the wallcovering over the fixture as you would a switch or outlet box. If the fixture or a protruding bracket remains, cut slits into the wallcovering. For a large protrusion, slit the covering from the nearest edge so it will slide around the obstacle. Work the covering into place around the box. Then lightly mark the perimeter of the box on the covering. Make a series of tension cuts that form a star from the center out to the perimeter of the box. This is called a star cut. Score the wallcovering into the opening with a 1-inch broad knife. Trim and smooth the remaining wallcovering around the box edge, and seam the slit back together.

## PERMANENT FIXTURES

Toilets, pedestal sinks, ceramic towel bars, and other items often can't be removed. When possible, remove parts, such as the toilet tank, to make wallpapering behind it easier. Adjust your layout to put full-width sheets of wallcovering on one side or both sides of the fixture, when possible. Use the star cut method as described for light fixtures to work around pipes.

## COVERING SWITCH AND OUTLET PLATES

Covering switchplates, outlet covers, and other panels with the wallcovering gives a room a professional appearance.
**1.** Match a scrap of the wallpaper to the area around the opening. Cut the scrap an inch larger than the switchplate on all sides and match it to the pattern again.
**2.** Clean the switchplate, then temporarily remount. Position the scrap over it, matching the pattern to the surrounding wall. Lightly mark the corners of the plate. Remove the scrap and plate from the wall. Mark the top on the back of the scrap and the plate.
**3.** Lay the piece of wallpaper face up on a cutting board. Lay the switch or outlet plate on top of it, using the corner marks to position it. Cut out the corners of the wallpaper to form top, bottom, and side tabs that will fold over the plate.
**4.** Coat the back of the wallpaper and the front side of the switch plate with spray adhesive; let dry.
**5.** Align the two top corners of the switchplate with the inside cut of the tabs

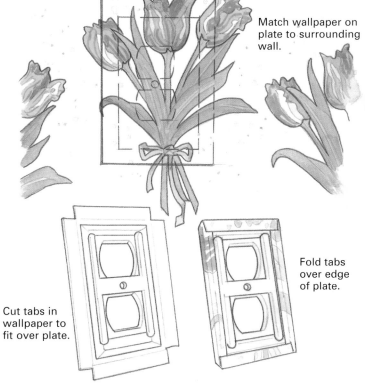

Match wallpaper on plate to surrounding wall.

Fold tabs over edge of plate.

Cut tabs in wallpaper to fit over plate.

on the scrap. Press the plate face firmly onto the back of the wallpaper.
**6.** Lay the plate with the wallpaper attached to it face down. Spray the back of the plate and the back of the tabs with spray adhesive. Let dry. Fold the tabs over onto the back of the plate.
**7.** In the opening, make a vertical cut parallel to the right side. Repeat for the left side. Join the two slits and trim to the edge of the opening on all sides.

## HEATING AND VENTILATING GRILLES

To prepare heating and ventilating grilles for covering, wash them with a solution of ½ cup of TSP in one gallon of warm water. Cover the grille to match the wall by following the procedure for switch and outlet plates. After adhering the wallpaper, cut out the slots in the grille with a knife.

You also can paint electrical plates and heating, air conditioning, and ventilating grilles with a color that matches or harmonizes with the wallpaper. Spray painting is the easiest and neatest way to do the job. If you have covered an electrical outlet plate, you can paint the face of the outlet itself to match the wallpaper better.

# WALLPAPERING IN SPECIAL SITUATIONS

Techniques for wallpapering ceilings, arches, and sloped walls are similar to basic techniques. Here are the steps:

## AROUND ARCHES

Install wallpaper in an archway the same way as in recessed windows, but wrap the sides only to the point where the curve begins. Cover the curve with a separate strip.

**1.** Let the drop hang over the opening. Hold the excess material taut with one hand while you cut from the outer edge to the wall at a point just below the curve. Wrap the flap around the side and smooth with your brush.

**WALLPAPERING AN ARCH**

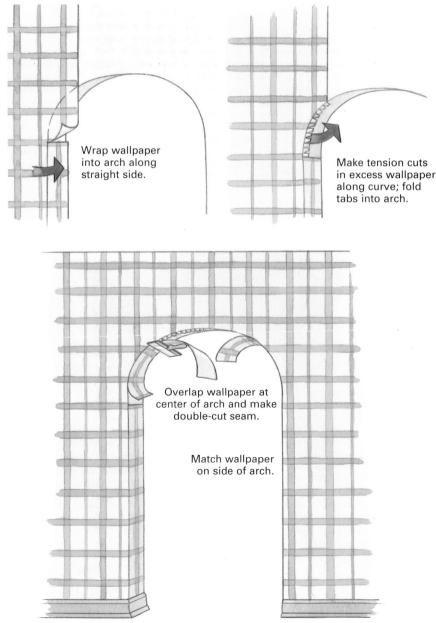

Wrap wallpaper into arch along straight side.

Make tension cuts in excess wallpaper along curve; fold tabs into arch.

Overlap wallpaper at center of arch and make double-cut seam.

Match wallpaper on side of arch.

**2.** Trim away the excess material within the curved opening to within ½ inch of the edge of the arch. Make a series of tension cuts at 1-inch intervals along the remaining excess material, stopping the cuts ⅛ inch short of the edge. Wrap the tabs into the arch.

**3.** Coat the interior of the arch with a lightweight spackling paste to hide the tabs. When the patching compound is dry, lightly sand with 120-grit sandpaper. Vacuum the dust. Apply a coat of latex primer-sealer.

**4.** Measure from the apex (top) of the arch to the edge of the wallcovering, then cut a new piece of wallpaper, with the correct match for each side of the arch. The width of the paper should be equal to the width of the arch plus 2 inches.

**5.** Align the wallpaper and hang from the bottom to the top, trimming, slitting, and wrapping it as you did the first drop.

**6.** Make a double-cut seam at the apex centerline. Using your broad knife as a guide, cut away the excess material at the bottoms of the strips so the strips form butt seams with the side flaps.

## CEILINGS

Whenever you wallpaper a ceiling, work along the shortest distance. For example, in a 12×15-foot room, Install the paper in 12-foot lengths.

**1.** Locate the center of the ceiling according to the focal-point wall and snap a chalk line to mark it. Lightly brush away excess chalk.

**2.** Coat the ceiling with a thin coat of wallpaper adhesive and let dry. This promotes better adhesion.

**3.** Wallpapering a ceiling always takes two people—one to hold the wallcovering while the other positions and smooths it. Start at the center of the ceiling. Otherwise, the procedure is the same as for walls. Allow a 2-inch margin on each end of each strip.

**4.** If matching patterns, hang the first ceiling sheet so that the pattern aligns with the pattern on the wall. Since they can match on only one wall, the match should be at the focal-point wall. Trim and smooth. Repeat for remaining sheets.

**WALLPAPERING ANGLED WALLS**

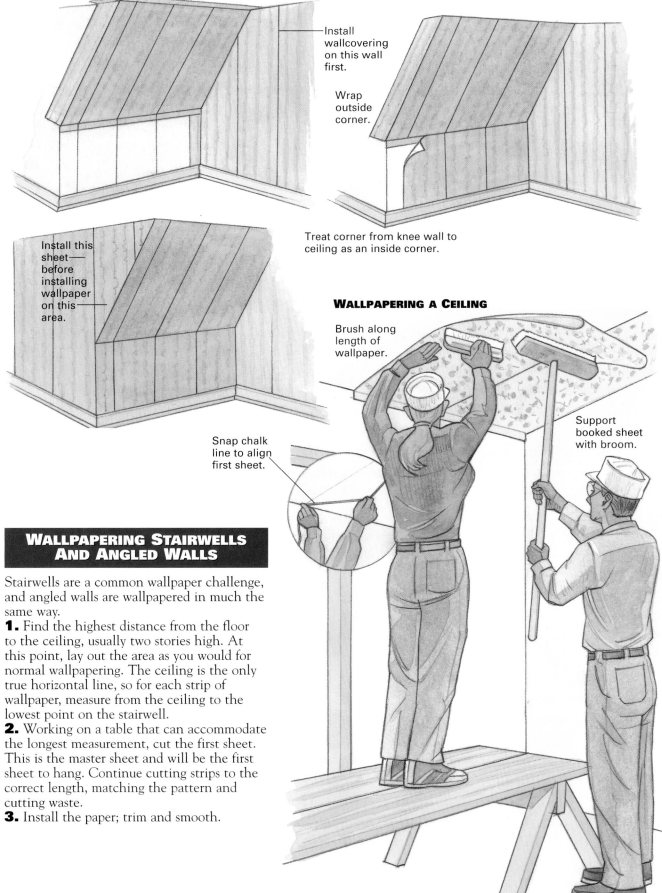

Install wallcovering on this wall first.

Wrap outside corner.

Install this sheet before installing wallpaper on this area.

Treat corner from knee wall to ceiling as an inside corner.

**WALLPAPERING A CEILING**

Brush along length of wallpaper.

Support booked sheet with broom.

Snap chalk line to align first sheet.

## WALLPAPERING STAIRWELLS AND ANGLED WALLS

Stairwells are a common wallpaper challenge, and angled walls are wallpapered in much the same way.

**1.** Find the highest distance from the floor to the ceiling, usually two stories high. At this point, lay out the area as you would for normal wallpapering. The ceiling is the only true horizontal line, so for each strip of wallpaper, measure from the ceiling to the lowest point on the stairwell.

**2.** Working on a table that can accommodate the longest measurement, cut the first sheet. This is the master sheet and will be the first sheet to hang. Continue cutting strips to the correct length, matching the pattern and cutting waste.

**3.** Install the paper; trim and smooth.

# DECORATIVE BORDERS

guidelines to mark the border's location on the wall. Measure from the ceiling rather than the floor.

## PREPARING THE WALL

If you hang the border separately, prepare the border area with a primer/sealer the same as for a wallcovering. Use the chalk lines as guides. If the wall is textured, line the edges of the border area with blue painter's masking tape, then float the area with two coats of joint compound.

## FRIEZE (CEILING-LINE) BORDERS

Measure the width of the border. Then measure this distance down from the ceiling at the corner of each wall, subtract ¼ inch, and mark placement. Snap a chalk line between the marks. The border's bottom edge will align with this line. Repeat on all the room's walls.

## DADO BORDERS

The bottom edge of a border usually sits 32 to 33 inches above the floor, the traditional chair-rail height. However, if your border is wide, center it on a line 33 inches above the floor to maintain attractive proportions in the room. You can hang a dado border at any height; it can be especially effective if it aligns with architectural features, such as windowsills, or borders chair-rail moldings.

Measure the width of the border. Then calculate the distance from the ceiling to the bottom of the border. Mark that distance at the corner of each wall, and snap a chalk line between the marks. The border's bottom edge will align with this line. Repeat on all the room's walls.

Borders along the ceiling, at chair-rail height, or around doors and windows add interest to a room and can help separate colors and textures. Careful installation of borders is a must; a wavy line will be obvious. A border at the ceiling line is called a frieze. One placed at chair-rail height is called a dado when there is no chair-rail molding.

## PLANNING THE LAYOUT

Most borders come in 5-yard rolls. Plan your lengths accordingly, allowing for the ¼ inch of material lost when you cut inside corners and for matching the pattern at ends, if necessary. Buy more than you need. Check the pattern number and dye lot for each package to make sure they match. Frieze, dado, and chair-rail borders start in the dead corner. Before you hang the border, check the material for flaws and back-roll it, the same as for a wallcovering. Then, snap horizontal

## PASTING AND BOOKING BORDERS

Book each strip in an accordion fold, paste to paste and pattern to pattern, and let it sit for three to five minutes. Roll the accordion fold, secure it with a rubber band, and place it in a zip-lock bag for 15 minutes. This makes the border easier to handle when hanging and allows the adhesive to activate. Repeat for remaining lengths of border. Follow instructions for working with prepasted or nonpasted wallcoverings. Prepasted borders also require complete immersion in water.

If the border will go over existing wallpaper, unfold one of the border lengths

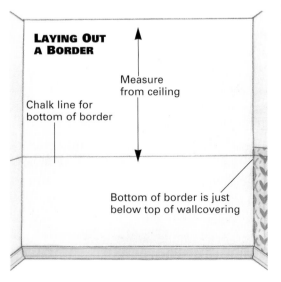

**LAYING OUT A BORDER**

Measure from ceiling

Chalk line for bottom of border

Bottom of border is just below top of wallcovering

### INSTALLING A BORDER

### DOUBLE-CUT SEAM FOR A DADO BORDER

and coat the back with a vinyl-to-vinyl adhesive, applying the adhesive as you hang the paper. Fold accordion style; repeat with remaining border pieces. Always wash the border and wall immediately because the vinyl-to-vinyl adhesive dries quickly and can ruin painted and papered surfaces.

### INSTALLING BORDERS

A border goes up easily if two people work together. One person feeds the border to the other, who smooths it into place. Work from left to right, unfolding an accordion-fold at a time and aligning the paper with the chalk line. Trim excess material along the edge of the ceiling. Smooth the border lengthwise, eliminating air pockets and helping the adhesive bond to the surface.

To match the pattern at the end, overlap a new length of border over the one already on the wall so that the pattern is aligned. Install the remaining paper to the inside corner and trim. Double-cut the wallpaper at the overlap; trim and remove excess material. Realign the pattern at the corner, trimming up to ¼ inch if needed, and continue around the room.

### DADO BORDER OVER WALLCOVERING

Snap a new guideline on the freshly installed wallcovering. Starting in the dead

corner, set the border's bottom edge on this line. Using a painting shield as a guide, make a double-cut seam along the border's bottom edge. Lift the border, remove the excess base covering, and smooth the border back into place. Repeat to double-cut the top edge of the border.

### MITERING CORNERS

When working around window or door molding, miter, or cut the corners on right angles, so the pattern appears to be continuous around the opening. Cross the borders at the corner, leaving 2 inches beyond the intersection. Double-cut through the borders on the diagonal, or intersection.

### CUTTING A CORNER MITER

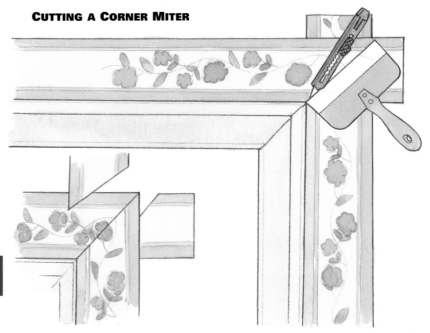

# REPAIR AND MAINTENANCE

## REPASTING SEAMS

Seams usually lift because of exposure to moisture or lack of adhesive. Pull back the seams to the point where they are secure, usually an inch inward. Mix four parts of seam repair adhesive or vinyl-to-vinyl adhesive with one part water. Using a small brush, apply a thin coat of adhesive to the wall and to the backsides of the open seams. When tacky to the touch, repeat the pasting procedure. This reinforces the strength of the adhesive. Let the adhesive get tacky, then use a wallpaper smoothing brush and gently tap the seams with the edge of the bristles. Pull the squeegee lightly over the seam to level. Wash off any adhesive residue from the paper.

## REPAIRING A GOUGE

**1.** Pull away damaged paper. Match a scrap of the original wallpaper to the wall, cutting the scrap 4 inches larger on all sides.
**2.** Activate and book, then lay the patch directly over the damaged area; smooth.
**3.** Working outside the damaged area, cut a football shape through both layers of wallpaper with a snap-off blade knife. Gently lift the excess material and the football-shaped patch from the wall; book and store in a resealable plastic bag.
**4.** Coat the damaged area with a solution of equal parts of hot water and liquid fabric softener until the damaged paper softens and lifts off the wall. Blot dry, then reposition the football-shaped patch within the damaged area and smooth.

## CLEANING WALLCOVERINGS

Dust all wallcoverings periodically to prevent dirt buildup. Most stains come out with a degreaser or spray-foam carpet and upholstery cleaner sold for home use. Test any cleaning product in an inconspicuous spot.
■ **WASHABLE WALLCOVERINGS:** Clean occasionally with a mild detergent solution (1 teaspoon of dishwashing detergent in a gallon of water) and cold water applied with a soft cloth or sponge. Treat stains before you wash the entire surface.
■ **SCRUBBABLE WALLCOVERINGS:** Scrub as often as necessary with a soft nylon brush and a mild detergent and warm water.
■ **NONWASHABLE WALLCOVERINGS:** Drycleaning with rubber wallpaper erasers will remove many marks. For more stubborn spots, blot the affected area with a sponge moistened with mild detergent and cold water. Don't scrub. Blot again with cold water and dry. If the stain still remains, ask your wallcovering dealer to recommend a spot remover. For overall griminess, use a commercial wallpaper eraser. Ask your dealer about sprays to make new nonvinyl wallcovering stain and dirt resistant.

## ELIMINATING BUBBLES

Most bubbles will disappear as the wallpaper dries. Here are some ways to remove ones that don't:
■ The easiest way to remove a dry bubble is

**DOUBLE-CUT PATCH REPAIR**

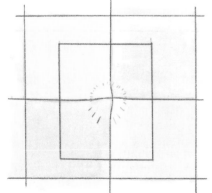
Match scrap of wallpaper to damaged area; mark position on wall.

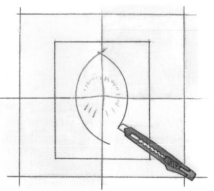
Place scrap of wallpaper over damaged area, make curved cuts through both layers around damage.

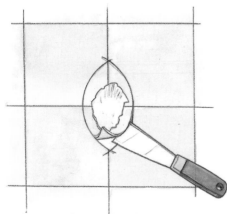
Remove damaged wallpaper.

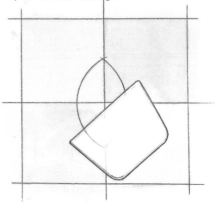
Paste patch from scrap of wallpaper into matching hole in original wallcovering.

**ELIMINATING LARGE BUBBLES**

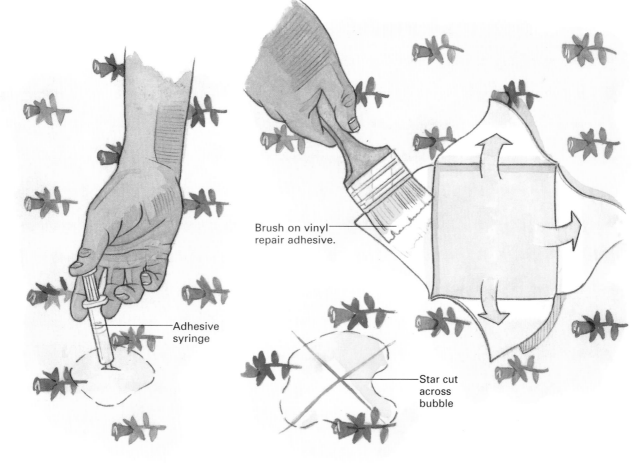

Adhesive syringe

Brush on vinyl repair adhesive.

Star cut across bubble

to make a double-cut patch repair, shown in the illustration on the opposite page.

■ Repair small bubbles with a paste syringe. Mix four parts of seam repair adhesive with one part water. Load the syringe, then lightly poke the needle at the edge of the bubble to release the air. Poke the bubble again and slowly shoot the thinned paste into the airspace. Use just enough to get it wet, and let it stand three to five minutes. Carefully press the wallcovering back onto the wall with a squeegee, gently working from the center to the perimeter of the bubble. Clean up any excess paste.

■ The V-cut method works well on medium-sized bubbles. To make the repair, cut a V through the wallpaper, 1 inch on the outside of the bubble. Gently lift the flap and apply the seam repair adhesive solution. Let dry, then reapply a second coat. Smooth and wash the wallpaper.

■ For large bubbles, use the V-cut method, substituting an X-cut through the bubble.

## WRINKLES

The best way to eliminate wrinkles is to reposition the sheet during installation. For wet wrinkles, you can also smooth the wrinkle with a squeegee while heating with a hair dryer. For dry wrinkles, preheat an iron at the polyester or permanent-press setting. Hold a wet terry washcloth over the crease and press the hot iron over the spot. Check the wrinkle every 15 seconds until it has softened but not pulled away from the wall. Gently smooth with the squeegee. Repeat the process until the wrinkle disappears. For permanent wrinkles, use the double-cut patch repair method.

## GAPPED SEAMS

To hide gapped seams, rub the dry seam with a pastel artist's chalk that matches the wallpaper. Blot away the excess chalk with a terry cloth towel.

# GLOSSARY

## A

**ACRYLIC:** A synthetic resin used as the binder in high-quality latex paint. Acrylic paints are durable and resist fading.

**ADHESION:** The ability of a paint or wallcovering to stick to the underlying surface without lifting, peeling, cracking, or flaking.

**ALKYD:** A synthetic resin used as a vehicle or solvent for oil-based paints.

**AMERICAN ROLL:** A measure of wallcovering. The American roll, sized in inches, yields about 36 square feet of material, about 25 percent more than a Euro roll. The wider American size results in fewer seams but is harder to handle. See also *Euro roll*.

## B

**BINDER:** The agent in a paint that adheres the pigment to the surface and imparts a particular sheen to the finish.

**BITE:** The ability of a paint or adhesive to adhere to a surface.

**BLANK STOCK:** See *liner paper*.

**BLUE MASKING TAPE:** A paint masking tape that can be removed from a surface without leaving residue or damaging the surface. Pressure along the edge can seal the tape to the surface to keep paint from creeping under it. See also *masking* and *masking tape*.

**BOLT:** A continuous roll of wallcovering equal in length to two or three single rolls.

**BOOKING:** A method of folding pasted wallcovering with the pasted side inside for easier handling.

**BORDER:** A narrow decorative strip of wallcovering applied at the top of a wall, at chair-rail height, along trim, or in another location as an accent.

**BREATHABLE:** A wallcovering that allows water vapor to pass through.

**BRUSH SPINNER:** A mechanical device that spins a paintbrush at high speed to remove thinners after cleaning. Can also be used for roller covers.

**BUTT-EDGE SEAM:** A wallcovering seam in which the edges of two adjoining drops butt together.

## C

**CEILING PAINT:** A thick, flat high-hiding paint made especially for ceilings. It can be tinted.

**CHAIR RAIL:** A decorative molding applied to a wall about 32 to 36 inches above the floor.

**CHALK LINE:** A straight line marked by snapping a chalk-covered string against a surface; also, the string used for marking a line in this way.

**COLOR RUN:** A batch of wallcovering printed at the same time. All rolls of wallcovering used in a room should come from the same color run because colors can vary between runs. Also called dye lot or run number.

**COLOR WASH:** A decorative finish created by applying a tinted glaze over a pale base coat.

**COMPANION WALLCOVERINGS:** Wallcoverings designed to coordinate. Some wallcoverings have companion fabrics too.

**CUTTING IN:** Applying a narrow band of paint in corners of walls and ceilings and along trim.

## D

**DADO:** A horizontal decorative border that divides a wall. See also *border*.

**DEAD CORNER:** An inconspicuous corner where the last sheet of wallpaper meets up with the first; the pattern often mismatches here.

**DEGLOSSING:** Roughing up the surface of a coat of paint to promote better adhesion of wallcovering or new paint. Deglossing can be mechanical (as in sanding) or chemical.

**DOUBLE-CUT SEAM:** A wallcovering seam in which two sheets are overlapped at the joining edges. A cut is made through the overlap, the waste pieces are removed, and the sheets are butted together.

**DROP:** A length of wallcovering cut to fit a particular space. A full drop runs from the ceiling to the baseboard on a wall, with an additional allowance for trimming. Also called a sheet.

**DROP MATCH:** A wallcovering design in which the pattern is staggered rather than running straight across. The same element in the pattern is at the top of alternate sheets. See also *straight-across match*.

**DYE LOT:** See *color run*.

## E

**EGGSHELL:** A soft paint sheen, named for its likeness to the surface of a fresh eggshell. Sometimes called satin or low-luster.

**ENAMEL:** A paint with high binder content that dries to a hard, smooth finish. Enamel sheens are usually gloss or semigloss.

**EURO ROLL:** A single roll of wallcovering sized in metric units; now the most common packaging for wallcovering. A roll yields about 29 square feet of wallcovering. It is narrower than the wallpaper packaged on American rolls. See also *American roll.*

## F

**FLAGGING:** Split ends on paintbrush bristles that help the brush hold more paint and apply it more evenly.

**FLAT:** A nonreflective paint sheen. Sometimes called matte.

**FRIEZE:** A decorative border applied along the top of a wall. See also *border.*

## G

**GLAZE:** A thin, transparent paint used for decorative effects. Also, to install glass in a window opening.

**GLAZING COMPOUND:** A puttylike material that holds glass in window openings and seals the edges of the openings.

**GLOSS:** A shiny paint sheen. Paint with a gloss sheen is usually enamel.

**HIDING:** A paint's ability to cover a previous coat of paint and prevent it from showing through. Also referred to as opacity.

**HVLP:** High-volume, low pressure; a kind of paint sprayer that reduces overspray.

## L

**LAP MARK:** A visible overlap in paint. Often a result of too much paint in the brush or roller or of painting over a dried edge.

**LAP SEAM:** A wallcovering seam in which one sheet overlaps another. This highly visible seam should be avoided.

**LATEX:** Water-based paint employing acrylic or vinyl resin or a blend of them as a binder.

**LEVEL:** Perfectly horizontal; parallel with the horizon. Also a tool for gauging level.

**LEVELING:** The ability of a paint to flow out smoothly on a surface so brush or roller marks don't show after the paint dries.

**LINER PAPER:** Paper or other material, also called blank stock, applied to imperfect walls to prepare the surface for wallcovering.

**LUSTER:** See *sheen.*

**MASKING:** Protecting an area or surface that isn't to be painted by covering it with tape or other material.

**MASKING TAPE:** A low-tack, crepe-backed tape made for paint masking. Ordinary beige masking tape left on a surface too long can leave residue. See also *blue masking tape.*

**MATTE:** Flat sheen.

**MINERAL SPIRITS:** Petroleum-base thinner for oil-base paints.

**MURIATIC ACID:** A dilute hydrochloric acid used for cleaning masonry. It is a hazardous material.

## P

**PAINTER'S TAPE:** Blue masking tape.

**PAINTING TAPE:** Masking tape with a micro-barrier edge to keep paint from seeping through or creeping under.

**PATTERN MATCH:** The alignment of wallcovering sheets so the pattern meets at the edges to create a continuous design around the room.

**PATTERN REPEAT:** The vertical distance between identical elements of a wallpaper pattern on a single sheet.

**PEELABLE:** A wallcovering in which the decorative surface can be separated from the backing. The backing should be removed from a surface before painting or hanging new wallcovering.

**PIGMENT:** The finely ground color materials that give paint its color.

# GLOSSARY
*continued*

**PLUMB:** A true vertical line that is best found with a plumb bob.

**PLUMB BOB:** A weight that is attached to a string or chalk line. When hanging free, it shows a true vertical line.

**PREPASTED:** Wallcovering with an adhesive coating applied at the factory. The adhesive is activated by submersion in water.

**PRETRIMMED:** Wallcoverings that come from the factory with the selvages removed. Also see *selvage*.

**PRIMER:** A base coat applied to help paint adhere to a surface. Latex or oil-based primers are available. Specialty primers are sold for use over metal and in other special situations.

## R

**RANDOM MATCH:** A wallcovering design in which the pattern doesn't align regularly along the edges. Random match wallcoverings are reverse hung. See *reverse hanging*.

**REPEAT:** The regular reoccurrence of pattern elements for wallcovering.

**RESIN:** A soluble substance that cures to a hard surface, used as a binder in paints. Most paint resins today are synthetic plastic materials, such as acrylic, vinyl, and urethane.

**REVERSE HANGING:** A method of hanging wallpaper in which alternate sheets are hung with the bottom of the sheet at the top of the wall. Employed for random match patterns.

**RUN NUMBER:** See *color run*.

## S

**SATIN:** A low-luster sheen.

**SCRUBBABILITY:** A paint's ability to stand up to repeated washing without fading or losing film thickness.

**SCRUBBABLE:** Wallcovering that can be cleaned with water, detergent, and a brush.

**SEALER:** An undercoat applied over porous or problem surfaces before painting. Sometimes called underbody.

**SELVAGE:** An unprinted band along the edge of some wallcoverings which must be trimmed off for hanging. Pretrimmed wallcoverings have no selvage.

**SEMIGLOSS:** A slightly reflective paint sheen.

**SHEEN:** The degree of light reflectivity of a painted surface. Also called luster or shine.

**SHEET:** See *drop*.

**SHINE:** See *sheen*.

**SLIDING CUT:** A method for cutting wallcovering by sliding a sharp knife along the edge of a surface beneath the wallcovering.

**SOLVENT:** The liquid used to thin paint or clean painting tools. Water is the solvent for latex paints; turpentine, paint thinner, or mineral spirits are solvents for oil-base paints. Also, the liquid component of paint.

**SPACKLING COMPOUND:** A paste for filling cracks, holes, and dents in wallboard, plaster, or painted woodwork.

**STAIN RESISTANT:** Wallcovering that has been treated so it will not absorb stains.

**STRAIGHT-ACROSS MATCH:** A wallcovering pattern that aligns horizontally from one sheet to the next. The same pattern element will appear at the top of each sheet. Also called straight match. See also *drop match*.

**STRIPPABLE:** A wallcovering that can be removed from the wall without first treating it with a wetting agent.

## T

**TEXTURED PAINT:** Thick paint, often containing granular material, that imparts texture to a surface.

**THINNER:** A liquid used to reduce the consistency of a paint for brushing, rolling, or spraying. See also *solvent*.

**TOOTH:** A surface coarseness that improves adherence of paint or adhesive.

**TSP:** Trisodium phosphate, a cleaning and deglossing agent; mix 1/4 cup per gallon of water.

**TURPENTINE:** A thinner for oil-base paints derived from natural pine resins.

## U-W

**UNDERBODY:** See *sealer*.

**UNIFORMITY:** Even appearance of color and sheen on a surface.

**UNTRIMMED:** Wallcovering with selvages attached. See *selvage*.

**VINYL:** A synthetic resin used as a binder in latex paints.

**WAINSCOT:** The lower part of wall when it has a different covering or finish than the upper part.

**WASHABLE:** Paint or wallcovering that can be cleaned with a mild detergent, water, and a sponge or rag.

**WET EDGE:** The undried edge of a painting stroke that helps blend the stroke into the adjacent stroke.

# INDEX

## METRIC CONVERSIONS

| U.S. Units to Metric Equivalents | | | Metric Units to U.S. Equivalents | | |
|---|---|---|---|---|---|
| To Convert From | Multiply By | To Get | To Convert From | Multiply By | To Get |
| Inches | 25.4 | Millimeters | Millimeters | 0.0394 | Inches |
| Inches | 2.54 | Centimeters | Centimeters | 0.3937 | Inches |
| Feet | 30.48 | Centimeters | Centimeters | 0.0328 | Feet |
| Feet | 0.3048 | Meters | Meters | 3.2808 | Feet |
| Yards | 0.9144 | Meters | Meters | 1.0936 | Yards |
| Square inches | 6.4516 | Square centimeters | Square centimeters | 0.1550 | Square inches |
| Square feet | 0.0929 | Square meters | Square meters | 10.764 | Square feet |
| Square yards | 0.8361 | Square meters | Square meters | 1.1960 | Square yards |
| Acres | 0.4047 | Hectares | Hectares | 2.4711 | Acres |
| Cubic inches | 16.387 | Cubic centimeters | Cubic centimeters | 0.0610 | Cubic inches |
| Cubic feet | 0.0283 | Cubic meters | Cubic meters | 35.315 | Cubic feet |
| Cubic feet | 28.316 | Liters | Liters | 0.0353 | Cubic feet |
| Cubic yards | 0.7646 | Cubic meters | Cubic meters | 1.308 | Cubic yards |
| Cubic yards | 764.55 | Liters | Liters | 0.0013 | Cubic yards |

To convert from degrees Fahrenheit (F) to degrees Celsius (C), first subtract 32, then multiply by $\frac{5}{9}$.

To convert from degrees Celsius to degrees Fahrenheit, multiply by $\frac{9}{5}$, then add 32.